Chemistry Matters!

THE PERIODIC TABLE

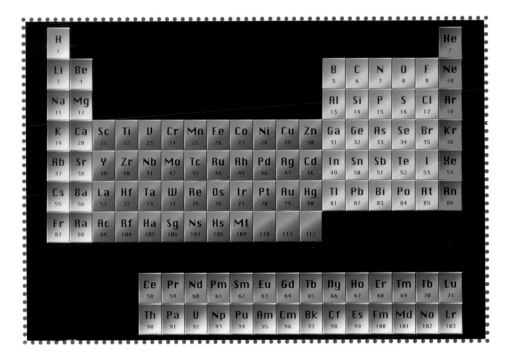

Volume 5

Leon Gray

GROLIER

an imprint of

www.scholastic.com/librarypublishing

About this set

Chemistry Matters! provides an intelligent and stimulating introduction to all areas of modern chemistry as reflected in current middle school and high school curricula. This highly visual set clearly explains principles and applications using dramatic photography and annotated artwork. Carefully chosen examples make the topic fun and relevant to everyday life. Panels detail key terms, people, events, discoveries, and technologies, and include "Try This" features, in which readers are encouraged to discover principles for themselves in safe step-by-step experiments at home or school. "Chemistry in Action" boxes give everyday examples of chemical applications.

First published in 2007 by Grolier, an imprint of Scholastic Library Publishing
Old Sherman Turnpike
Danbury, Connecticut 06816

© 2007 The Brown Reference Group plc

Volume ISBN 0-7172-6199-9; 978-0-7172-6199-4
Set ISBN 0-7172-6194-8; 978-0-7172-6194-9

Library of Congress Cataloging-in-Publication Data

Chemistry matters!
     v. cm.
  Includes bibliographical references and index.
  Contents: v.1. Atoms and molecules—v.2. States of matter—v.3. Chemical reactions—v.4. Energy and reactions—v.5. The periodic table—v.6. Metals and metalloids—v.7. Nonmetals—v.8. Organic chemistry—v.9. Biochemistry—v.10. Chemistry in action.
  ISBN 0-7172-6194-8 (set : alk. paper)—ISBN 0-7172-6195-6 (v.1 : alk. paper)—ISBN 0-7172-6196-4 (v.2 : alk. paper)—ISBN 0-7172-6197-2 (v.3 : alk. paper)—ISBN 0-7172-6198-0 (v.4 : alk. paper)—ISBN 0-7172-6199-9 (v.5 : alk. paper)—ISBN 0-7172-6200-6 (v.6 : alk. paper)—ISBN 0-7172-6201-4 (v.7 : alk. paper)—ISBN 0-7172-6202-2 (v.8 : alk. paper)—ISBN 0-7172-6203-0 (v.9 : alk. paper)—ISBN 0-7172-6204-9 (v.10 : alk. paper)
  1. Chemistry—Encyclopedias.
  QD4.C485 2007
  540—dc22
                                        2006026209

For The Brown Reference Group plc

Project Editor: Wendy Horobin
Editors: Paul Thompson, Tom Jackson, Susan Watt, Tim Harris
Designer: Graham Curd
Picture Researchers: Laila Torsun, Helen Simm
Illustrators: Darren Awuah, Mark Walker
Indexer: Ann Barrett
Design Manager: Sarah Williams
Managing Editor: Bridget Giles
Production Director: Alastair Gourlay
Editorial Director: Lindsey Lowe
Children's Publisher: Anne O'Daly

Academic Consultants:

Dr. Donald Franceschetti, Dept. of Physics, University of Memphis
Dr. Richard Petersen, Dept. of Chemistry, University of Memphis

Printed and bound in Singapore.

Picture Credits

Front cover: NASA

Airbus: 42; **Alamy:** Andre Scale 60, Visual Arts Library (London) 12b; **ARS:** David Nance 48b; **Corbis:** James L. Amos 33, Archivo Incongrafico S.A. 11b, Lester V. Bergam 28c, 28cl, 28cr, 28l, 28r, Bettmann 31, Tim Davis 49, Andre Fichte 58, Paul A. Souders 21; **Getty Images:** Richgitz/Stringer; **NASA:** 4; **Photos.com:** 10, 18, 29, 34, 40, 44, 47, 48t, 52, 53, 54; **SCETI:** 17, 19, 51c, 51l, 51r; **Science and Society:** Science Museum 16l, 16r, 39, 43r, Science Museum/Pictorial 22; **Shutterstock:** Kevin Britland 43l, W. H. Chow 6, Mihaicalin 27; **Science Photo Library:** 15c, 15t, 61, Andrew Lambert Photography 15b, Lawrence Berkeley 63, George Bernard 11t, Martin Bond 57t, 59, Vaughan Fleming 20, Roberto De Gugliemo 26, ISM 23, Ted Kinsman 14, Russell Knightly 50, Mehau Kulyk TP, 5, Sam Ogeden 36, David Parker 64, 65, Philippe Psaila 57b, Sheila Terry 13, U.S. Dept. of Energy 62, Dirk Wiersma 9, Charles D. Winters 12t, 38, David Wunuk 30; **Still Pictures:** Jean-Leo Dugast 56; **Topham:** UPP 46.

Contents

1 Atoms and Elements

Atoms are the key to how the periodic table is arranged. Each atom has a structure that defines the properties and place in the table of every element.

The periodic table adorns the pages of every chemistry textbook and the walls of every high-school laboratory. This simple chart is a "dictionary" for every chemist. It defines the elements, of which everything in the universe is made, in measurable quantities, such as atomic number and atomic mass. It is arranged in a way that highlights similarities between the different elements.

Elements are formed by the stars. As stars burn they create new elements. When a star explodes as a supernova, these new elements are flung out into space. The red outer ring of this supernova shows the presence of oxygen and neon.

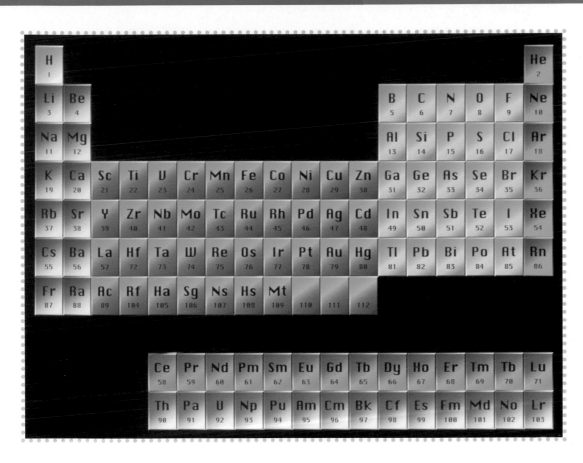

◄ *The periodic table sets out all the known elements in order of their atomic number. Elements fall into vertical and horizontal families; the members of each family all have similar chemical and physical properties.*

MAKING UP MATTER

The building blocks of matter are called atoms. These tiny particles are so small that scientists can only see them by using powerful microscopes. Almost all atoms consist of even smaller particles called protons, neutrons, and electrons. The protons and neutrons are found in the dense nucleus at the center of the atom. The electrons revolve around the nucleus in a series of layers called electron shells.

A chemical element consists of atoms with the same number of protons in their nucleus. The number of protons is what gives an element its atomic number. For example, an atom of the element hydrogen (chemical symbol H) has only 1 proton in its nucleus. An atom of uranium (chemical symbol U) always

Key Terms

• **Atomic number:** The number of protons in the nucleus of an atom.
• **Chemical symbol:** A shorthand way of writing the name of a chemical element.
• **Element:** A substance made up of only one type of atom.

has 92 protons in its nucleus. Therefore the atomic number of hydrogen is 1, and the atomic number of uranium is 92.

ARRANGING ELECTRONS
Each proton has a positive electrical charge. Neutrons have no electrical charge. Each electron has a negative electrical charge. Atoms are electrically neutral because the number of electrons and protons is the same, so the positive and negative charges cancel out. Thus, a hydrogen atom always has 1 electron, while a uranium atom has 92 electrons.

Electrons revolve around the nucleus in a series of layers, called electron shells, similar to the way in which planets orbit the sun. For this reason, this description of the atom is known as the planetary model.

The electron shells are a series of energy levels, with all the electrons in the same shell having similar energy (*see* vol. 1: p. 36–41). An atom can have up to seven shells. Each electron shell can hold only a limited number of electrons. For example, the first shell can hold up to two electrons, the second shell can hold

▲ *The Golden Pavilion temple in Kyoto, Japan, built in 1955 as a replacement for the 1397 original, is covered in gold leaf. Gold was one of the elements known to early chemists. Many performed experiments to try to turn other substances into gold, which has always been highly prized.*

up to eight electrons, the third shell can hold up to 18 electrons, while the fourth shell can hold up to 32 electrons.

FORMING IONS

An atom can gain or lose electrons to form what is called an ion. Adding or removing the electrons does not change the atom into the atom of another element. An ion is simply an electrically charged form of the atom. A hydrogen atom may lose its electron to form a hydrogen ion. The hydrogen ion is written as H^+. The plus sign means that the hydrogen ion has a positive charge. It has this positive charge because the negative electron was removed from the atom. This leaves just one positive proton in the atom, resulting in an electrical charge of +1.

Molecules and compounds

A compound is made up of different elements that are joined by chemical bonds. Water is a compound made of the elements hydrogen and oxygen. Two hydrogen atoms link with one oxygen atom, resulting in one molecule of water. The chemical symbol for hydrogen is H and oxygen is O, but the formula for the water molecule is H_2O. This shows that each molecule of water is made from two hydrogen atoms and one oxygen atom.

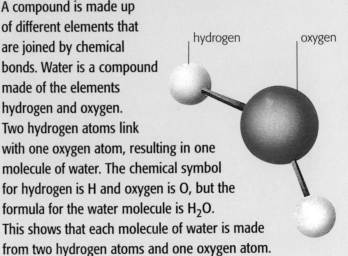

hydrogen   oxygen

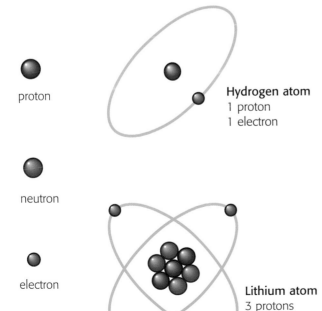

proton

neutron

electron

Hydrogen atom
1 proton
1 electron

Helium atom
2 protons
2 electrons
2 neutrons

Lithium atom
3 protons
3 electrons
4 neutrons

Beryllium atom
4 protons
4 electrons
5 neutrons

◄ *Atoms are made up of protons, electrons, and neutrons. Atoms always have the same number of protons and electrons, but may sometimes have extra neutrons in the nucleus. The first four elements in the periodic table are hydrogen, helium, lithium, and beryllium.*

A Closer LOOK

Shells and orbitals

The planetary model of the atom came from the pioneering work of scientists in the late 19th and early 20th centuries. However, it soon became clear that atoms were far more complicated. In 1926, Austrian physicist Erwin Schrödinger (1887–1961) came up with the laws of quantum mechanics. In quantum mechanics, electrons are spread around the nucleus in a series of clouds. Each cloud is called an orbital. Orbitals are rather like the electron shells of the planetary model, but the shapes vary with the size of the atom. However, the math used to describe orbitals is complex.

STABLE ATOMS

Atoms are stable if the outermost electron shell is full. The atoms of some elements share electrons with the atoms of other elements to make them stable. Other atoms give electrons to the atoms of other elements to become stable. Sharing or transferring electrons results in the formation of a chemical bond between the atoms.

ISOTOPES

The number of protons is always the same for each element, but the number of neutrons may be different. For

▶ Many atoms have isotopes, which are versions of the atom that have more than the usual number of neutrons in the nucleus. Hydrogen has two isotopes called deuterium and tritium. Deuterium has one neutron in the nucleus and tritium has two. Carbon usually has six protons and six neutrons in its nucleus, but one of its isotopes has eight neutrons. This isotope is called carbon-14, which indicates the total number of protons and neutrons it contains.

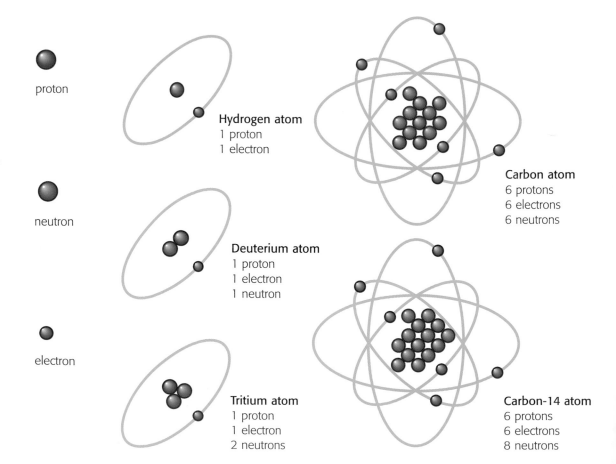

proton

neutron

electron

Hydrogen atom
1 proton
1 electron

Deuterium atom
1 proton
1 electron
1 neutron

Tritium atom
1 proton
1 electron
2 neutrons

Carbon atom
6 protons
6 electrons
6 neutrons

Carbon-14 atom
6 protons
6 electrons
8 neutrons

*··· **Key Terms** ···*

- **Atomic mass:** The average of all the mass numbers of an element's isotopes.
- **Compound:** A substance made up of a number of different elements joined by chemical bonds.
- **Ion:** An atom that has gained or lost one or more electrons. Atoms that lose electrons form positive ions. Atoms that gain electrons form negative ions.
- **Isotope:** An atom of an element that has a different number of neutrons in its nucleus.
- **Mass number:** The sum of the protons and neutrons in an atom's nucleus.
- **Molecule:** A particle made up of two or more atoms of the same or different elements joined by chemical bonds.

example, a carbon atom (chemical symbol C) always contains six protons in its nucleus. Most carbon atoms contain six neutrons in the nucleus, but some have seven neutrons, and a few have eight neutrons. These different versions of the same element are called isotopes. The number of protons and neutrons in the nucleus of an atom is called the mass number. Most elements are a mixture of different isotopes. Since the mass number of each isotope is different, scientists take an average of all the mass numbers. The result is the element's official atomic mass.

▶ *The mineral calcite is a compound made from the elements calcium, oxygen, and carbon. Calcite, or calcium carbonate, is one of the most common minerals on Earth.*

See ALSO ...
What Is Matter?, Vol. 1: pp. 4–15.
Introducing Elements, Vol. 1: pp. 16–23.

2 Identifying Elements

Elements such as gold, mercury, and sulfur have been known for thousands of years, but people did not know that they were elements. Scientists now recognize 116 elements and there may be more waiting to be discovered.

More than 2,000 years ago, scholars from ancient Greece used the words *atom* and *element* to describe the basic building blocks of matter. Thales of Miletus (c. 625–547 B.C.E.) believed that water was the fundamental substance of which everything in the universe was made. Heracleitus (c. 540–480 B.C.E.) thought that it was fire. Later, Aristotle (384–322 B.C.E.) suggested that everything consisted of a mixture of four different "elements." These were earth, water, air, and fire.

This image represents the four "elements" of the ancient world: Fireworks represent fire, the river represents water, and earth and air are represented by the land and surrounding air respectively.

used to make tools and weapons. Iron was first used in present-day Turkey around 1400 B.C.E., marking the start of the Iron Age. Iron is harder than bronze, so the tools and weapons made from iron were much stronger.

THE AGE OF ALCHEMY
New elements started to be discovered from about the 13th century. Early chemists, called alchemists, did many experiments in their search for the philosopher's stone. This mystical substance was thought to turn base metals such as lead into valuable gold and silver. The search for the philosopher's stone was in vain, but alchemists found many important

In fact, many elements were already known by the time of the ancient Greeks. Gold and silver are found as pure elements in nature. These metals were being used from before 5000 B.C.E. Carbon and sulfur were also known since they are found as pure elements in nature.

Some metals were vital in the development of human civilization. The Bronze Age, which dates from around 4300 B.C.E., is a period in history when people mixed copper and tin to make an alloy called bronze. The bronze was then

◀ *Greek philosopher Aristotle thought that everything was made of only four elements: earth, air, fire, and water.*

▼ *These Iron Age axes were found by archaeologists in Spain. The Iron Age in Europe did not begin until around 800 B.C.E. The Iron Age occurred at different times at different places, depending on when techniques for producing iron were discovered.*

Tools and Techniques

Electrolysis

Scientists often use a chemical process called electrolysis to separate elements from their compounds. Electrolysis involves passing electricity through a compound. The compound then splits into positive and negative ions, which move toward a pair of conductors called electrodes. The electrodes are the substances used to conduct the electricity into and out of the compound. Positive ions collect at the negative electrode (cathode), and negative ions collect at the positive electrode (anode). At each electrode, the ions either gain or lose electrons to become atoms again.

▲ The electrolysis of tin chloride leaves tin on the cathode (right) and chlorine gas at the anode (left). This process can be used as a method for plating steel with tin.

compounds and a few new elements along the way. Among them were antimony (1450) and zinc (1526) and also arsenic, which had been known about since ancient times but was first isolated as an element in 1250.

German alchemist Hennig Brand (c. 1630–1710) discovered another new element in 1669. He collected his urine in a bottle and concentrated it into a white, glowing solid that he named phosphorus. A few years later, Irish chemist Robert Boyle (1627–1691) read about Brand's experiment. Boyle realized that true

▼ This painting depicts the discovery of the element phosphorus by Hennig Brand. The light from the glass vessel is supposed to be caused by the glow from phosphorus, though the artist has exaggerated its effect.

elements were substances such as Brand's phosphorus, because phosphorus could not be broken down into one of Aristotle's four "elements."

NEW DISCOVERIES

During the 18th century, many scientists did experiments to break down substances into simpler substances. A range of new elements were discovered, such as cobalt, chromium, nickel, and nitrogen. By the end of the 18th century, scientists had identified about 33 elements.

In the early 1800s, English chemist Humphry Davy (1778–1829) found a new way to break down different substances. He passed electricity through compounds to split them up into elements in a process now called electrolysis. In this way, Davy discovered potassium, sodium, calcium, and barium. Other elements were discovered using a technique called spectroscopy, which is the study of objects based on characteristic patterns of light, called spectra, they

Profile

Humphry Davy

Humphry Davy (1778–1829) was one of the most influential chemists of his time. Born in Penzance, Cornwall, in the United Kingdom, he began his career as an apprentice to an apothecary (an early druggist). In 1799, while he was still a laboratory assistant, Davy discovered the anesthetic effects of laughing gas (nitrous oxide). After he moved to the Royal Institution in 1801, Davy became interested in the new science of electrolysis. Using this method he discovered the elements sodium, potassium, calcium, boron, magnesium, chlorine, strontium, and barium. Davy also speculated that electrolysis worked on a principle of separation by the electrical charge of the element, where positive ions would go to the negative electrode and negative ions to the positive electrode. This theory led to a large-scale expansion of the alkali industry, which made use of the technique.

Davy made significant contributions to other areas of chemistry, particularly its applications in agriculture, the leather tanning industry, and mineralogy. Two of his most famous inventions were the miner's safety lamp, an arc lamp for illumination, and an electrolytic process for removing salt from seawater.

▲ Humphry Davy tests his miner's safety lamp. Prior to this invention, the flame on miners lamps risked igniting methane in mines. Use of the safety lamp saved the lives of thousands of miners from explosions.

emit. Using spectroscopy, scientists discovered new elements such as cesium, helium, and xenon.

Two more breakthroughs came before the end of the 19th century. The first was the discovery of the noble gases. Noble gases have full outer electron shells (see pp. 6–7) and are largely unreactive, which is why they were not identified for so long. British scientists Lord Rayleigh (1842–1919) and William Ramsay (1852–1916) identified argon in 1894. By 1898 Ramsay had discovered three more noble gases—krypton, neon, and xenon. The second breakthrough came from the work of Polish-born scientist Marie Curie

(1867–1934) and her French husband, Pierre Curie (1859–1906). Their studies of radioactivity led to the discovery of radium and polonium in 1898 and helped other scientists identify many more new elements in the 20th century.

Many scientists did important work that helped create the periodic table. Some are given credit for their contribution to modern chemistry, while others have largely been forgotten.

French chemist Antoine-Laurent Lavoisier (1743–1794) made the first list of elements in his book *Elementary Treatise of Chemistry* (1789). The list included hydrogen, mercury, oxygen,

▼ *These colors are the spectrum produced by the element bromine. Each element produces a characteristic spectrum and this fact enables chemists to discover which elements are present in a sample.*

Tools and Techniques

Spectroscopy

Spectroscopy is a technique that is used to identify elements. It works by analyzing the wavelengths of light or other forms of electromagnetic radiation, such as X-rays, microwaves, or radio waves, given off by a substance. All elements give off electromagnetic radiation at specific wavelengths. Many of these wavelengths fall in the range of the visible spectrum, which we see as colors. This effect is best demonstrated by a prism, which splits white light into a rainbow. Each color has its own wavelength and is bent by the prism at a specific angle.

At its simplest, a spectroscope works by collecting the light that is emitted by a substance and passing it through a prism or grating that bends the light into its separate wavelengths. By measuring the angles between the wavelengths and comparing them with a known spectral chart for each element, scientists can determine what the unidentified substance is made from. This technique is very useful in astronomy, where it is used to discover what elements are contained in stars and nebulas.

wavelength

◄ *Wavelength is measured as the distance between two equal parts (such as two peaks) of a wave.*

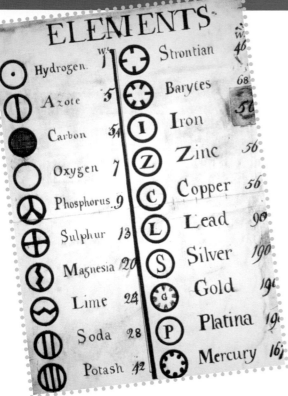

◀ In 1808 John Dalton produced a list of elements and their atomic mass, and gave each element a circular symbol.

▼ Johann Döbereiner arranged some of the elements into groups of three according to their similarities. One group included chlorine, bromine, and iodine.

example, Döbereiner grouped three soft and reactive metals—lithium, sodium, and potassium. He also grouped three pungent and harmful elements: chlorine, bromine, and iodine. As well as having similar chemical properties, the atomic mass of the middle element in each triad was the average of the other two elements. Döbereiner published his "law of triads" in 1829.

By 1843 German chemist Leopold Gmelin (1788–1853) added elements to Döbereiner's triads. Gmelin added fluorine to the triad of chlorine, bromine, and iodine, making one group of four,

nitrogen, phosphorus, sulfur, and zinc. However, Lavoisier made some mistakes. For example, he put lime on his list of elements. Chemists now know that lime is a compound of calcium and oxygen.

In the early 19th century, British scientist John Dalton (1766–1844) wrote *A New System of Chemical Philosophy*. In his book, Dalton talked about particles called atoms—the building blocks of matter. He suggested that the atoms of different elements had different atomic masses (*see* p. 9). Different elements then combine in exact amounts to make compounds.

DÖBEREINER'S TRIADS

German chemist Johann Döbereiner (1780–1849) arranged elements into groups of three, called triads. The members of each triad had similar chemical properties. For

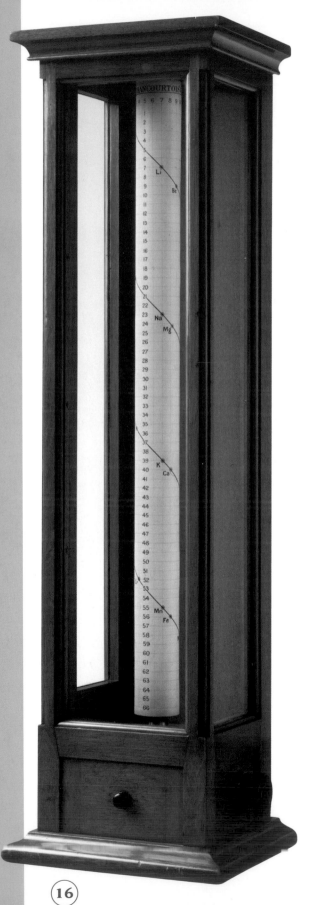

◀ *In 1862 Bèguyer de Chancourtois produced a periodic table based on atomic mass. He arranged the elements in a spiral around a cylinder. At the center of this system was the element tellurium. This table is therefore called a telluric screw.*

▼ *In the 19th century many attempts were made to produce an accurate periodic table. In 1888 English scientist William Crookes produced this spiral periodic table. The table shows the chemical relationships between the elements.*

called a tetrad. Gmelin recognized that oxygen, sulfur, selenium, and tellurium had similar chemical properties and so grouped them together.

A NEW ORDER

In 1860 Italian chemist Stanislao Cannizzaro (1826–1910) published a list of the atomic masses of the known elements. The list was announced at a science meeting in Karlsruhe, Germany.

Many scientists attended the meeting. Among them was a geology professor from France, Alexandre-Emile Bèguyer de Chancourtois (1820–1886). Using Avogadro's atomic masses, de Chancourtois came up with one of the earliest periodic tables. He arranged the known elements in order of atomic mass. De Chancourtois placed the elements in a spiral around a cylinder. He noticed that Gmelin's tetrad—oxygen, sulfur, selenium and tellurium—formed a

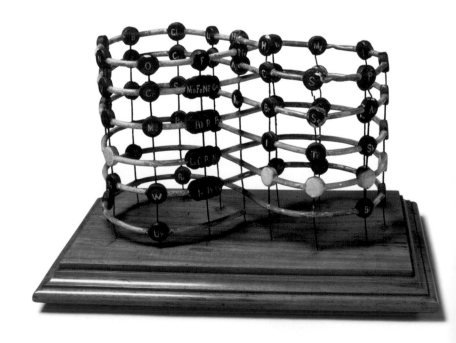

vertical column on the spiral. De Chancourtois called his arrangement of elements the "telluric spiral," because tellurium fell in the center of the spiral.

THE LAW OF OCTAVES

In 1864 English chemist John Alexander Reina Newlands (1837–1898) listed the known elements in order of increasing atomic mass. He found that an element in this order shared its chemistry with elements eight places before and after it. He called this pattern his law of octaves, because it was like the eight musical notes in an octave. Newlands announced his law of octaves in 1866, but chemists did not treat his discovery seriously.

IGNORED CONTRIBUTIONS

The year 1864 was a busy time for chemists trying to organize the elements. First, English chemist William Odling (1829–1921), president of the Chemical Society of London, published a chart of known elements in order of atomic mass. Odling did not organize all the known elements, and he left gaps to suggest

Profile

John Newlands

John Alexander Reina Newlands was born in London, England, on November 26, 1837. His father was a religious minister from Scotland, and his mother's family came from Italy. Newlands studied under his father at home and then attended the Royal College of Chemistry in 1856. Later he worked as an industrial chemist.

When Newlands came up with his "law of octaves," his fellow scientists dismissed the work as nonsense. When the periodic table eventually became accepted, scientists realized that Newlands's law was right. Newlands eventually got the recognition he deserved in the form of a Royal Society Davy Medal in 1882. He died of influenza in 1898.

▲ As well as producing the theory of octaves, John Newlands introduced improvements for sugar-refining processes.

some unknown elements. Like Newlands's table, Odling's table was ignored, but is no less important. In the same year, German chemist Julius Lothar Meyer (1830–1895) published a table of about 49 elements. In his table, Meyer listed the elements by valence. Valence is the usual number of bonds an atom can form with other atoms. Eventually, Meyer revised the list in order of atomic mass, but with elements of similar valence grouped in columns. Meyer had created the first periodic table, but he took too long to publish his findings. A young Russian chemist named Dmitry Ivanovich Mendeleyev beat him to it.

Key Terms

- **Atomic mass:** The sum of the number of protons and neutrons in an atom's nucleus.
- **Electrolysis:** A chemical reaction caused by passing an electric current through a liquid.
- **Four elements:** In ancient times people believed that everything in the universe was made of four elements: earth, air, fire, and water.

See ALSO ...
What Is Matter?, Vol. 1: pp. 4–15.

3 The Modern Table

The modern periodic table was devised by Russian chemist Dmitry Ivanovich Mendeleyev (1834–1907). New elements have since been added, but the basic structure of Mendeleyev's table remains the same.

Legend has it that Mendeleyev came up with the periodic table when he was playing a card game called solitaire. There is little historical evidence, however, to back up this account. It is clear that Mendeleyev arranged the table using a list of atomic masses produced in 1860 at a science meeting in Karlsruhe, Germany. Atomic mass is the sum of the number of protons and neutrons in an atom's nucleus. Mendeleyev believed that atomic mass was the most important property of an element, though we now know that elements are defined by their atomic number—the number of protons in an atom's nucleus (*see* pp. 5–6).

It is likely that Mendeleyev came up with the periodic table while he was

Lightbulbs typically contain the noble gas argon. The noble gases rarely react with other elements and so were the last group of elements to be discovered and the last group to be added to the periodic table.

writing a textbook, *The Principles of Chemistry* (1868–1870). In this book, Mendeleyev grouped elements with similar physical and chemical properties. For example, he grouped the halogens (Group 17 elements) in one chapter and the alkali metals in another chapter.

Mendeleyev was grouping elements with the same valence. Valence is a measure of the number of bonds an atom can form with other atoms. Valence is

▼ *Dmitry Ivanovich Mendeleyev was one of the most influential scientists of his time. His periodic table revolutionized chemistry and helped scientists discover new elements.*

determined by the number of electrons in the outer electron shell of an atom (*see* pp. 6–7). Atoms share or transfer these outer electrons, forming chemical bonds with other atoms. The halogens have similar properties because they all have seven electrons in the outer electron shell, and they all readily accept one electron to form bonds with other elements. In contrast, the alkali metals share physical and chemical properties

Profile

Mendeleyev

Dmitry Ivanovich Mendeleyev was born in Tobol'sk, Siberia, on February 8, 1834. From an early age, it was clear that he was a talented scientist. His mother tried to find him a place at university, but Mendeleyev was turned away from the Russian universities of Moscow and St. Petersburg. Finally, in 1850, he enrolled as a trainee science teacher at the Institute of St. Petersburg and graduated with distinction. In 1855 he took a job as a science teacher at Simferopol near the Black Sea. A year later, he returned to St. Petersburg and completed a master's degree. In 1859 he traveled abroad to work in laboratories in Europe. On his return in 1861, Mendeleyev focused on an academic career and eventually became a chemistry professor at St. Petersburg University. In 1869 he published his first version of the periodic table. His final years were spent as director of the bureau of weights and measures in St. Petersburg. Mendeleyev received many awards from universities around the world. In 1906 he came within one vote of receiving the Nobel Prize in chemistry. He died in St. Petersburg in 1907.

A Closer LOOK

What's in a name?

There is no right or wrong way to spell Mendeleyev's name in English. In Russian, words are written using the Cyrillic alphabet, for which there is no literal English translation. Consequently, you might see Mendeleyev's name written as Mendelev, Mendeleev, Mendeleeff, or Mendelayev.

because they have just one electron in the outer electron shell, and they all readily donate the electron to form bonds with other elements.

As Mendeleyev tried to group similar elements, a pattern emerged. He arranged the 61 known elements in a chart in order of increasing atomic mass (*see* below). Mendeleyev found that elements with the same valence appeared in the same columns of the chart. Mendeleyev had outlined the basic structure of the periodic

table. He published his findings in 1869 and produced a revised table in 1871 that placed the elements into eight groups.

FILLING THE GAPS

One of Mendeleyev's great achievements was to move elements to new places in the chart despite upsetting the order suggested by atomic mass. In this way, he kept the order of elements by valence. Perhaps the greatest achievement, however, was to describe elements that

▲ *Scientists think that the blue color in aquamarine gemstones is caused by small quantities of scandium. Before scandium was discovered, Mendeleyev predicted its existence using his periodic table.*

◄ *Mendeleyev's second periodic table of 1871. Mendeleyev's work enabled chemists to identify families of elements with similar chemical properties. Mendeleyev arranged the elements by atomic mass (the sum of the protons and neutrons). Today, the elements are arranged according to their atomic number (proton number).*

	Gruppe I.	Gruppe II.	Gruppe III.	Gruppe IV.	Gruppe V.	Gruppe VI.	Gruppe VII.	Gruppe VIII.
Typische Elemente	H 1 Li 7	Be 9,4	Bo 11	C 12	N 14	O 16	F 19	
Reihe 1	Na 23	Mg 24	Al 27,3	Si 28	P 31	S 32	Cl 35,5	
- 2	Ka 39	Ca 40	—44	Ti 50(?)	V 51	Cr 52	Mn 55	Fe 56, Co 59, Ni 56, Cu [63
Reihe 3	(Cu 63)	Zn 65	—68	—72	As 75	Se 78	Br 80	
- 4	Rb 85	Sr 87	(Yt 88)(?)	Zr 90	Nb 94	Mo 96	—100	Ru 104, Rh 104, Pl 106, [Ag 108
Reihe 5	(Ag 108)	Cd 112	In 113	Sn 118	Sb 122	Te 125	J 127	
- 6	Cs 133	Ba 137	—137	Ce 138(?)	—	—	—	
Reihe 7	—	—	—	—			—	
- 8	—	—	—		Ta 183	W 184	—	Os 199 (?), Jr 198, Pt [197, Au 197
Reihe 9	(Au 197)	Hg 200	Tl 204	Pb 207	Bi 208	—	—	
- 10	—	—	—	Th 232	—	Ur 240	—	
Höchste salz-bild. Oxyde	R^2O	R^2O^2 od. RO	R^2O^3	R^2O^4 o. RO^2	R^2O^5	R^2O^6 o. RO^3	R^2O^7	R^2O^8 od. RO^4
Höchste H-Verbindung				RH^4	RH^3	RH^2	RH	(R^2H) (?)

had not yet been discovered. Mendeleyev was convinced of the natural order of the periodic table. His table, however, contained gaps, and Mendeleyev reasoned that these gaps must represent elements not yet discovered. He even predicted the physical and chemical properties of these missing elements.

One of these gaps occurred below aluminum in Mendeleyev's table and so he named it eka-aluminum (*eka* is Sanskrit for "one" and eka-aluminum is one place from aluminum in the periodic table). This element was discovered by French scientist Paul-Emile Lecoq de Boisbaudran (1838–1912) in 1875. He called it gallium in honor of his country (*Gallia* is the Latin name for France). In 1879 Swedish chemist Lars Frederick Nilson (1840–1899) discovered the element that

Mendeleyev called eka-boron. Nilson named this element scandium in honor of Scandinavia. In 1886, German chemist Clemens Winkler (1838–1904) discovered Mendeleyev's eka-silicon. Winkler named it germanium in honor of Germany. In all cases, the properties of the new elements matched Mendeleyev's predictions.

A NEW GROUP OF GASES
In 1895 English chemist John William Strutt, later Lord Rayleigh (1842–1919), and Scottish chemist William Ramsay (1852–1916) identified a gas that they called argon. The new element did not seem to fit anywhere in Mendeleyev's periodic table. Ramsay thought that similar gases to argon must exist and so set about trying to find them. In 1895, he produced helium. In 1898 he carried out

▼ *Arc welding uses an electric current to produce a sparklike electric arc that fuses metals together by melting them. Argon is sometimes used in arc welding because it is an inert gas and so does not react with the molten metal, resulting in a more stable arc.*

▲ William Ramsay won the Nobel Prize for chemistry in 1904 for his work on the discovery of the noble gases.

This experiment revealed that the center of an atom consists of a dense, positively charged nucleus. Two years after Rutherford's discovery, English physicist Henry Moseley (1887–1915) used a machine called an electron gun to fire electrons at the atoms of different elements. He found that the elements gave off X-rays—high-energy radiation with short wavelengths. These X-rays had characteristics that depended on the number of protons in the nucleus. Moseley wrote down the proton number (now called atomic number) of many different elements. He then made a chart of all the known elements in order of increasing proton number. Following in Mendeleyev's footsteps, Moseley also left gaps in his chart, predicting the existence of two new elements. These missing elements were later discovered and are called technetium and promethium. Moseley also corrected some of the errors associated with a table arranged by atomic mass.

THE PROBLEM WITH ATOMIC MASS

Atomic mass is a measure of the number of protons and neutrons in the nucleus of an atom. The atoms of an element always contain the same number of

further research with English chemist Morris Travers and together they identified neon, krypton, and xenon. Four years later, Mendeleyev revised his periodic table. He put the new group of gases in a group at the end of the periodic table. Chemists originally named this family of elements "inert gases," because they could not be made to react with other elements. Inert gases are now called noble gases because they do react in certain circumstances.

ATOMIC NUMBER

In 1911 New Zealand-born British physicist Ernest Rutherford (1871–1937) carried out an important experiment.

Key Terms

- **Atomic mass:** The number of protons and neutrons in a nucleus.
- **Atomic number:** The number of protons in an atom's nucleus.

- **Noble gases:** A group of gases that rarely react with other elements.
- **Valence:** A measure of the number of bonds an atom can form with other atoms.

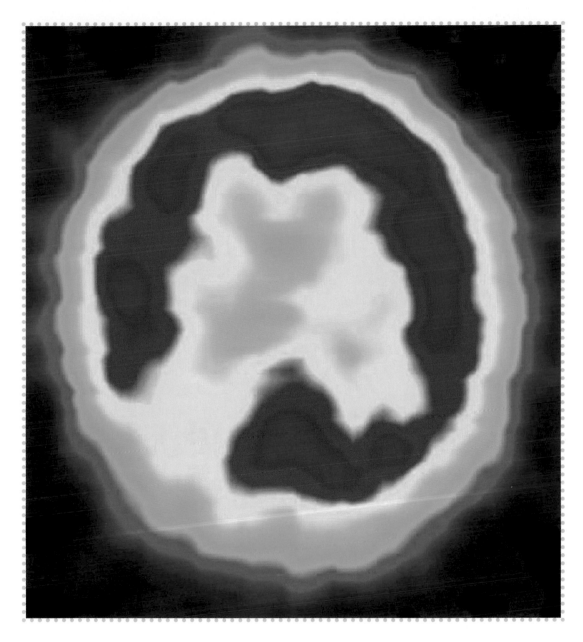

◀ *An isotope of technetium is commonly used in some scans that enable doctors to see inside a patient's body. This scan shows a person with Alzheimer's disease. The break in the red ring (lower left) shows the area of the brain that is degenerating.*

protons, but they may have different numbers of neutrons. These different versions of atoms are called isotopes (*see* pp. 8–9). Atomic number is the basic property on which the periodic table is best organized, not atomic mass. Fortunately for Mendeleyev, who did not know about protons and neutrons, atomic mass and atomic number increase roughly in proportion.

THE MODERN PERIODIC TABLE
The last major change to the periodic table came in the middle of the 20th century. American physicist Glenn Seaborg (1912–1999) and his colleagues discovered 11 new elements with atomic numbers greater than that of uranium (atomic number 92). Seaborg rearranged the periodic table to accommodate these new elements.

See also ...
- *Introducing Elements,* Vol. 1: pp. 16–23.
- *Radioactivity,* Vol. 1: pp. 56–65.
- *Noble Gases,* Vol. 7: pp. 60–65.

Reading the Table

The periodic table organizes all the chemical elements into a simple chart according to the physical and chemical properties of their atoms.

The periodic table arranges elements in order of increasing atomic number. The rows are called periods and the columns are called groups. In general, elements in the same column have similar chemical properties. The arrangement of the electrons in the atoms of elements determines the structure of the periodic table itself.

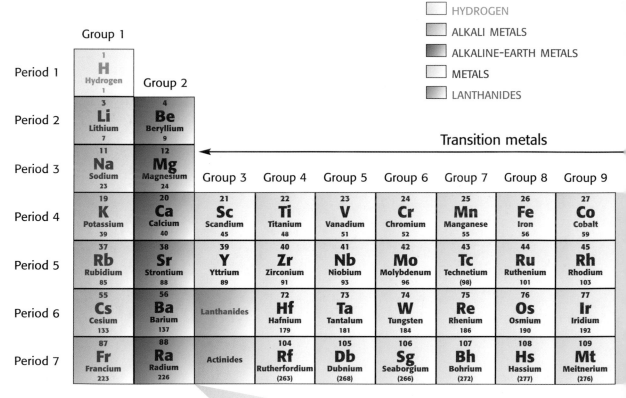

- HYDROGEN
- ALKALI METALS
- ALKALINE-EARTH METALS
- METALS
- LANTHANIDES

Transition metals

	Group 1	Group 2		Group 3	Group 4	Group 5	Group 6	Group 7	Group 8	Group 9
Period 1	1 **H** Hydrogen 1									
Period 2	3 **Li** Lithium 7	4 **Be** Beryllium 9								
Period 3	11 **Na** Sodium 23	12 **Mg** Magnesium 24								
Period 4	19 **K** Potassium 39	20 **Ca** Calcium 40		21 **Sc** Scandium 45	22 **Ti** Titanium 48	23 **V** Vanadium 51	24 **Cr** Chromium 52	25 **Mn** Manganese 55	26 **Fe** Iron 56	27 **Co** Cobalt 59
Period 5	37 **Rb** Rubidium 85	38 **Sr** Strontium 88		39 **Y** Yttrium 89	40 **Zr** Zirconium 91	41 **Nb** Niobium 93	42 **Mo** Molybdenum 96	43 **Tc** Technetium (98)	44 **Ru** Ruthenium 101	45 **Rh** Rhodium 103
Period 6	55 **Cs** Cesium 133	56 **Ba** Barium 137	Lanthanides	72 **Hf** Hafnium 179	73 **Ta** Tantalum 181	74 **W** Tungsten 184	75 **Re** Rhenium 186	76 **Os** Osmium 190	77 **Ir** Iridium 192
Period 7	87 **Fr** Francium 223	88 **Ra** Radium 226	Actinides	104 **Rf** Rutherfordium (263)	105 **Db** Dubnium (268)	106 **Sg** Seaborgium (266)	107 **Bh** Bohrium (272)	108 **Hs** Hassium (277)	109 **Mt** Meitnerium (276)

rare-earth elements
- Lanthanides
- Actinides

57 **La** Lanthanum 39	58 **Ce** Cerium 140	59 **Pr** Praseodymium 141	60 **Nd** Neodymium 144	61 **Pm** Promethium (145)
89 **Ac** Actinium 227	90 **Th** Thorium 232	91 **Pa** Protactinium 231	92 **U** Uranium 238	93 **Np** Neptunium (237)

33	— Atomic (proton) number
As	— Chemical symbol
Arsenic	— Element name
75	— Atomic mass

- ACTINIDES
- NOBLE GASES
- NONMETALS
- METALLOIDS

�◄ *The classic representation of the periodic table sets the elements out into 18 groups arranged in 7 rows. Rows are arranged in order of increasing atomic number, from left to right. All the members of a group show related properties in the way they react chemically with other groups in the table. All the gases except hydrogen are at the upper right of the table, and the metals are all in the left and center. Metals constitute the bulk of the elements. Most of the radioactive elements are in the actinide group.*

Group 13	Group 14	Group 15	Group 16	Group 17	Group 18
					2 **He** Helium 4
5 **B** Boron 11	6 **C** Carbon 12	7 **N** Nitrogen 14	8 **O** Oxygen 16	9 **F** Fluorine 19	10 **Ne** Neon 20
13 **Al** Aluminum 27	14 **Si** Silicon 28	15 **P** Phosphorus 31	16 **S** Sulfur 32	17 **Cl** Chlorine 35	18 **Ar** Argon 40

Group 10	Group 11	Group 12					
28 **Ni** Nickel 59	29 **Cu** Copper 64	30 **Zn** Zinc 65	31 **Ga** Gallium 70	32 **Ge** Germanium 73	33 **As** Arsenic 75	34 **Se** Selenium 79	35 **Br** Bromine 80	36 **Kr** Krypton 84
46 **Pd** Palladium 106	47 **Ag** Silver 108	48 **Cd** Cadmium 112	49 **In** Indium 115	50 **Sn** Tin 119	51 **Sb** Antimony 122	52 **Te** Tellurium 128	53 **I** Iodine 127	54 **Xe** Xenon 131
78 **Pt** Platinum 195	79 **Au** Gold 197	80 **Hg** Mercury 201	81 **Tl** Thallium 204	82 **Pb** Lead 207	83 **Bi** Bismuth 209	84 **Po** Polonium (209)	85 **At** Astatine (210)	84 **Rn** Radon (222)
110 **Ds** Darmstadtium (281)	111 **Rg** Roentgenium (280)	112 **Uub** Ununbium (285)	113 **Uut** Ununtrium (284)	114 **Uuq** Ununquadium (289)	115 **Uup** Ununpentium (288)	116 **Uuh** Ununhexium (292)		

elements awaiting official names

62 **Sm** Samarium 150	63 **Eu** Europium 152	64 **Gd** Gadolinium 157	65 **Tb** Terbium 159	66 **Dy** Dysprosium 163	67 **Ho** Holmium 165	68 **Er** Erbium 167	69 **Tm** Thulium 169	70 **Yb** Ytterbium 173	71 **Lu** Lutetium 175
94 **Pu** Plutonium (244)	95 **Am** Americium (243)	96 **Cm** Curium (247)	97 **Bk** Berkelium (247)	98 **Cf** Californium (251)	99 **Es** Einsteinium (252)	100 **Fm** Fermium (257)	101 **Md** Mendelevium (258)	102 **No** Nobelium (259)	103 **Lr** Lawrencium (260)

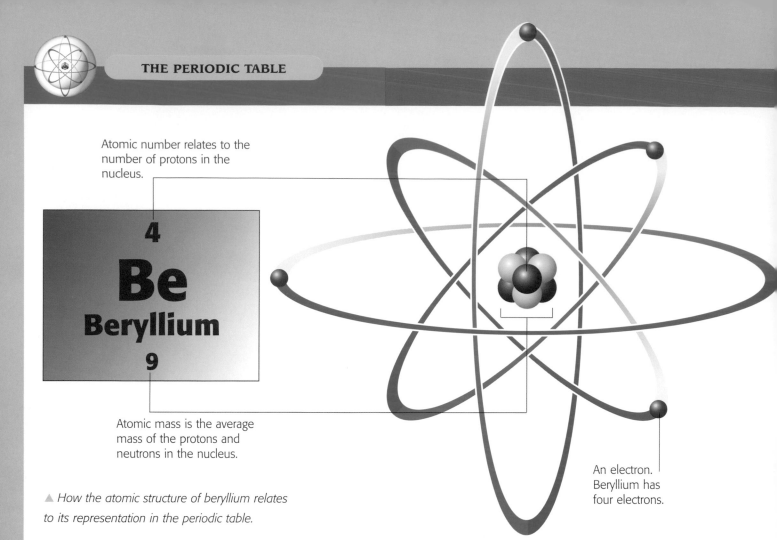

Atomic number relates to the number of protons in the nucleus.

4
Be
Beryllium
9

Atomic mass is the average mass of the protons and neutrons in the nucleus.

An electron. Beryllium has four electrons.

▲ *How the atomic structure of beryllium relates to its representation in the periodic table.*

THE BASIC ORDER

The atomic number of an element is the number of protons in the nucleus of one atom of that element. A hydrogen atom always has one proton in its nucleus. The atomic number is 1, so hydrogen takes first place in the periodic table. A helium atom always has two protons in the nucleus. Its atomic number is 2, so it is second in the table, after hydrogen. A uranium atom always has 92 protons in its nucleus. The atomic number is 92 so uranium takes 92nd position.

Arranging elements in order of their atomic number eliminates the problems Mendeleyev had when he organized the elements in order of atomic mass. From left to right along a row of the periodic table, the atomic number rises by one whole unit for each element. Elements in

◀ *One of the chief sources of the element beryllium is a mineral made up of aluminum, silicon, and oxygen. One of its crystalline forms is aquamarine, which is cut into a sparkling pale blue gemstone. Emerald is another form of this mineral.*

3	4	5	6	7	8	9	10
Li	**Be**	**B**	**C**	**N**	**O**	**F**	**Ne**
Lithium	Beryllium	Boron	Carbon	Nitrogen	Oxygen	Fluorine	Neon
7	9	11	12	14	16	19	20

lower rows have higher atomic numbers than elements above. Chemists can be absolutely sure that there are no missing atomic numbers and no missing elements.

WHAT DOES IT SHOW?

Each box of the periodic table represents one element. The box must show the element's atomic number, its name, and its chemical symbol. Aside from this, there are no strict rules. The atomic mass of the element is usually included, since it reflects the history of the periodic table. Some versions may have up to 20 data sets for each element, including, for example, electron arrangements (*see* pp. 6–7) and whether the element is normally a solid, liquid, or gas at standard conditions of temperature and pressure. In many modern tables the elements are also shaded according to type, showing which are metals, nonmetals, and metalloids. Other tables

have individual shading for specific groups of elements, for example, one color for the alkali metals, one for the alkaline earths, one for the halogens, and so on. Not all are arranged in straight rows or columns. Some are arranged in spirals or in shapes that represent relationships between the elements' chemical properties.

ROWS ARE CALLED PERIODS

The seven main rows of the periodic table are called periods. Hydrogen and helium make up Period 1. Next come the two short periods of eight elements: Period 2 starts with lithium (atomic number 3) and ends with neon (10). Period 3 starts with sodium (11) and ends with argon (18). Then come the two long periods, each of 18 elements. Period 4 starts with potassium (19) and ends on krypton (36). Period 5 starts with rubidium (37) and ends with xenon (54).

▲ *Period 2 of the periodic table begins with lithium and ends with neon. As the elements progress along the row, their chemical nature changes from metallic (Li and Be) to metalloid (B), to nonmetallic (C), and finally gaseous (N, O, F, and Ne).*

▼ *Plants and animals rely on three of the Period 2 elements to live and grow. Carbon and the gases nitrogen and oxygen make up about 90 percent of the dry weight of all living organisms.*

Key Terms

- **Group:** A column of related elements in the periodic table.
- **Metalloid:** An element that has some of the properties of metals and some of the properties of nonmetals.
- **Period:** A row of elements across the periodic table.

Some of the elements in the long periods 4 and 5 are called transition metals. In Period 4, the transition metals start with scandium (21) and end with zinc (30). In Period 5, the transition metals start with yttrium (39) and end with cadmium (48).

Period 6 is a very long row of 32 elements, starting with cesium (55) and ending with radon (86). In most modern periodic tables, Period 6 is reduced to 18 elements by moving 14 elements, called the lanthanides, to the bottom of the

▼ *Flame tests, where a sample is burned in a flame, can be used to identify elements. This series shows the Group 1 alkali metals. From left: lithium, sodium, potassium, rubidium, and cesium.*

table. Not only does the table then fit on a normal size page, it also allows elements with similar valence to be placed in the same columns. (Valence depends on the number of electrons in the outer shell and determines the reactivity of the element; *see* pp. 16–17.) So the transition metals in Period 6 end with mercury (80), which lies directly below cadmium, the last transition metal in Period 5.

Period 7 is an incomplete row, ending with the artificial element 116—the last element to be officially recognized. Artificial elements do not occur in nature but have been created in laboratories by scientists (*see* p. 65). Period 7 is another very long period of 32 elements that will be completed when element 118 is discovered. Period 7 is also shortened by moving 14 elements, called the actinides, to the bottom of the table.

COLUMNS ARE CALLED GROUPS

Elements with the same number of electrons in their outer electron shells are usually found in columns called groups (right). Chemists place hydrogen at the top of Group 1, but it is not really

1
H
Hydrogen
1

3
Li
Lithium
7

11
Na
Sodium
23

19
K
Potassium
39

37
Rb
Rubidium
85

55
Cs
Cesium
133

87
Fr
Francium
223

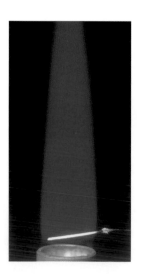
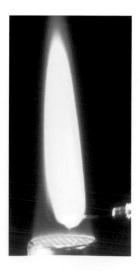
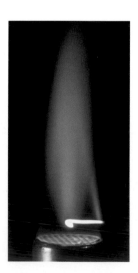

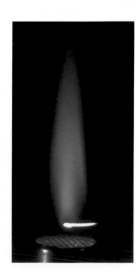

part of the group. Group 1 actually starts with lithium (3) and ends with francium (87). Unlike hydrogen, the Group 1 elements are soft, strong, metals. All of them react with water to form alkaline solutions (*see* vol. 6: pp. 16–17). For this reason, the Group 1 elements are called the alkali metals.

The Group 2 elements start with beryllium (4) and end with radium (88). The Group 2 elements are known as the alkaline-earth metals. These metals also react with water to form alkaline solutions. The word *earth* comes from an old term used to describe the compounds formed when the Group 2 metals reacted with oxygen.

Groups 3 to 12 comprise the transition metals in the center of the periodic table and rare-earth metals at the bottom of the table. The chemistry of the transition metals is less predictable than that of the alkali and alkaline-earth metals. Some transition metals, such as cobalt (27) and iron (26), form many different colored

compounds. Others, such as gold (79) and platinum (78), hardly react at all and can be found as pure metals in nature.

Groups 13, 14, 15, and 16 form groups of elements that do not seem as clearly related as the previous groups. Metalloids (metal-like elements), such as boron (6) and silicon (14), and many solid

▲ *Transition metals form compounds of many colors. That makes them very useful in the glass industry where this property helps make colored marbles.*

A home for hydrogen

In most versions of the periodic table, hydrogen is put above the alkali metals in Group 1 at the top left of the periodic table. There is a problem with this, however, because hydrogen is a gas and all the Group 1 elements are metals. In other versions of the table, hydrogen can be found above the halogens in Group 17. Sometimes, hydrogen appears in both groups, and sometimes it is left to float freely at the top of the table. In fact, hydrogen is a unique element that no one really knows where to place.

nonmetals, such as phosphorus (15) and sulfur (16), are found in groups 13 through 16. The halogens make up Group 17. This group starts with fluorine (9) and ends with astatine (85). All halogens are reactive, and fluorine is the most reactive of all the elements.

The Group 18 elements start with helium (2) and end with radon (86). These gases had not been discovered when Mendeleyev's original table was published in 1869. Mendeleyev added them to the end of his revised table in 1902. The Group 18 elements do not react with many other elements. For this reason, they are known as the noble, or inert, gases.

NUMBERING CONVENTIONS

From the top to the bottom of the periodic table, the periods (rows) are simply numbered 1 through 7. The numbering of the groups is more problematic. There are three systems for numbering the groups. The first uses Roman numbers (I, II, III, IV, V, and so on). The second system uses

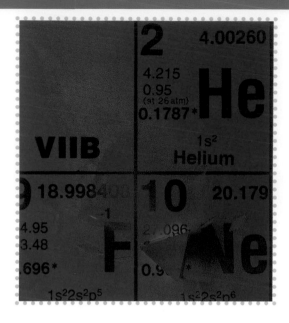

◄ *The light from a helium–neon laser shines on the two squares (He and Ne) that represent these elements in the periodic table. Helium and neon are the first two elements in the noble gases, which comprise the Group 18 elements.*

a combination of Roman numbers and the letters A and B. In 1985, the International Union of Pure and Applied Chemistry (IUPAC) replaced the traditional Roman numbers and letters. The new system uses the Arabic numbers 1 to 18, starting with the alkali metals (Group 1) and ending with the noble gases (Group 18). You may still see the traditional system used in modern textbooks because many chemists did not want to change the Roman number convention.

Chemical symbols

A chemical symbol is the shorthand way of writing an element's name. Chemical symbols are used in writing chemical equations. The symbol itself consists of either one or two letters. Usually, the symbol is the first letter of the element's common name. So, hydrogen is "H," and boron is "B." Sometimes the symbol is the first letter of the element's Latin name. For example, potassium is "K," after its Latin name *kalium*. Inevitably, the names of some elements start with the same letter, so a symbol may consist of two letters. Only the first letter is a capital. So, helium is "He," while barium is "Ba." Iron has the chemical symbol Fe for its Latin name *ferrum*.

A Closer LOOK

An element by any other name

Deciding what to call an element has posed a challenge to scientists throughout the centuries. Of the elements that have been known longest, most countries have their own names for elements such as gold, silver, or mercury. For example, France and Greece call nitrogen *azote*, and Germany uses *Sauerstoff* for oxygen. Some use versions of the Latin names and are very similar. Silver is *argentum* in Latin, which is changed to *argento* in Italian and *argent* in French.

To avoid confusion in international trade and ensure that scientists of all nations can talk about the same element without any risk of misidentification, element names have been standardized. The body that oversees this process is the International Union of Pure and Applied Chemistry, or IUPAC. Among its rulings are that internationally aluminum and cesium should be known by their British spellings "aluminium" and "caesium" but that sulfur should take the U.S. spelling (not sulphur).

With new elements still being synthesized in the laboratory, IUPAC is also involved in the naming process. Often the new element has been found by two or more laboratories and they may have different ideas about what to call it. There have been many arguments over what to call the heavy elements with atomic numbers between 104 and 111. These have now been agreed as rutherfordium (104), dubnium (105), seaborgium (106), bohrium (107), hassium (108), meitnerium (109), darmstadtium (110), and roentgenium (111). Elements beyond these are known by a Latinized form of their atomic number–ununbium (112), ununtrium (113), ununquadium (114), and so on.

Most of the elements are named after places or people. The places are usually where the element was first discovered or the discoverer's country. Those named after people honor famous scientists or characters from mythology. A few are named after astronomical objects.

◀ *Helios, the Greek sun god after whom helium is named.*

Elements named after places

Americium–the Americas
Californium–the state of California
Darmstadtium–Darmstadt, Germany
Europium–Europe
Francium–France
Hafnium–*Hafnia*, Latin for Copenhagen
Holmium–*Holmia*, Latin for Stockholm
Lutetium–*Lutetia*, Latin for Paris
Magnesium–Magnesia, Greece
Polonium–Poland
Strontium–Strontian, Scotland
Ytterbium, Yttrium–Ytterby, Sweden

Elements named after people or gods

Bohrium–Niels Bohr
Curium–Pierre and Marie Curie
Einsteinium–Albert Einstein
Fermium–Enrico Fermi
Helium–Helios, the Greek sun god
Mendelevium–Dmitri Mendeleyev
Niobium–Niobe, a woman in Greek mythology
Nobelium–Alfred Nobel
Selenium–Selene, Greek goddess of the moon
Thorium–Thor, the Scandinavian god of thunder
Tellurium–*Tellus*, Latin name for Earth
Vanadium–Vanadis, a Scandinavian goddess

softest metals hardest metals less hard metals

Halogens become more reactive up the group.

metalloids

1 H Hydrogen 1																	2 He Helium 4
3 Li Lithium 7	4 Be Beryllium 9											5 B Boron 11	6 C Carbon 12	7 N Nitrogen 14	8 O Oxygen 16	9 F Fluorine 19	10 Ne Neon 20
11 Na Sodium 23	12 Mg Magnesium 24											13 Al Aluminum 27	14 Si Silicon 28	15 P Phosphorus 31	16 S Sulfur 32	17 Cl Chlorine 32	18 Ar Argon 40
19 K Potassium 39	20 Ca Calcium 40	21 Sc Scandium 45	22 Ti Titanium 48	23 V Vanadium 51	24 Cr Chromium 52	25 Mn Manganese 55	26 Fe Iron 56	27 Co Cobalt 59	28 Ni Nickel 59	29 Cu Copper 64	30 Zn Zinc 65	31 Ga Gallium 70	32 Ge Germanium 73	33 As Arsenic 75	34 Se Selenium 79	35 Br Bromine 80	36 Kr Krypton 84
37 Rb Rubidium 85	38 Sr Strontium 88	39 Y Yttrium 89	40 Zr Zirconium 91	41 Nb Niobium 93	42 Mo Molybdenum 96	43 Tc Technetium (98)	44 Ru Ruthenium 101	45 Rh Rhodium 103	46 Pd Palladium 106	47 Ag Silver 108	48 Cd Cadmium 112	49 In Indium 115	50 Sn Tin 119	51 Sb Antimony 122	52 Te Tellurium 128	53 I Iodine 127	54 Xe Xenon 131
55 Cs Cesium 133	56 Ba Barium 137		72 Hf Hafnium 179	73 Ta Tantalum 181	74 W Tungsten 184	75 Re Rhenium 186	76 Os Osmium 190	77 Ir Iridium 192	78 Pt Platinum 195	79 Au Gold 197	80 Hg Mercury 201	81 Tl Thallium 204	82 Pb Lead 207	83 Bi Bismuth 209	84 Po Polonium (209)	85 At Astatine (210)	86 Rn Radon (222)
87 Fr Francium 223	88 Ra Radium 226		104 Rf Rutherfordium (263)	105 Db Dubnium (268)	106 Sg Seaborgium (266)	107 Bh Bohrium (272)	108 Hs Hassium (277)	109 Mt Meitnerium (276)	110 Ds Darmstadtium (281)	111 Rg Roentgenium (280)	112 Uub Ununbium (285)	113 Uut Ununtrium (284)	114 Uuq Ununquadium (289)	115 Uup Ununpentium (288)	116 Uuh Ununhexium (292)		

mostly gases

Alkali metals become more reactive down the group.

rare-earth metals

57 La Lanthanum 39	58 Ce Cerium 140	59 Pr Praseodymium 141	60 Nd Neodymium 144	61 Pm Promethium (145)	62 Sm Samarium 150	63 Eu Europium 152	64 Gd Gadolinium 157	65 Tb Terbium 159	66 Dy Dysprosium 163	67 Ho Holmium 165	68 Er Erbium 167	69 Tm Thulium 169	70 Yb Ytterbium 173	71 Lu Lutetium 175
89 Ac Actinium 227	90 Th Thorium 232	91 Pa Protactinium 231	92 U Uranium 238	93 Np Neptunium (237)	94 Pu Plutonium (244)	95 Am Americium (243)	96 Cm Curium (247)	97 Bk Berkelium (247)	98 Cf Californium (251)	99 Es Einsteinium (252)	100 Fm Fermium (257)	101 Md Mendelevium (258)	102 No Nobelium (259)	103 Lr Lawrencium (260)

▲ *Arranging the elements in the periodic table reveals certain trends across periods and up and down groups, such as hardness, reactivity, and physical state.*

Key Terms

- **Boiling point:** The temperature at which a liquid turns into a gas.
- **Melting point:** The temperature at which a solid turns into a liquid.
- **Standard conditions:** Normal room temperature and pressure.

TRENDS IN THE TABLE

Today, the periodic table consists of 116 elements in seven periods and 18 groups. At standard conditions (room temperature and pressure), two of these elements are liquids (bromine and mercury), 11 are gases, and the rest are solids. Aside from hydrogen and mercury, the gases and liquids are on the right of

Melting and boiling points across Period 2

			Lithium	Beryllium	Boron	Carbon	Nitrogen	Oxygen	Fluorine	Neon
						Element				
melting point		°F	357	2,349	3,769	6,381	−346	−361	−363	−415
		°C	180.5	1,287	2,076	3,527	−210	−218	−219	−248
boiling point		°F	2,448	4,476	7,101	7,281	−320	−297	−306	−411
		°C	1,342	2,469	3,927	4,027	−196	−183	−188	−246

the table. Most metals are on the left-hand side and bottom of the table. The metalloids form a diagonal line, from boron to tellurium, on the right-hand side of the table. Most nonmetals, such as carbon, oxygen, nitrogen, and the halogens, are on the right and top of the table (aside from the noble gases). Thus there is a general trend for elements to become less metal-like from left to right across a period.

The alkali metals in Group 1 are soft metals with low melting points. The alkaline-earth metals in Group 2 are harder and have higher melting points than the metals of Group 1. Moving from left to right across the periods, elements gradually get harder and have higher melting and boiling points (*see* table on p. 32). These properties peak at the center of the table. The hardness, melting, and boiling points then begin to fall again.

TRY THIS

Color in the periodic table

Search for a few different versions of the periodic table on the Internet. Compare them to the one printed in this book. Which table do you think works best? Use a printer to make some copies of the periodic tables you have found. You could also take a photocopy of the periodic table in this book. Then shade in one color all the elements that are metals. Then shade in all the gases in another color. Shade the remaining boxes that are neither metals nor gases using a different color. You might need to do some research before you start coloring in the boxes to find out which elements are metals, which are gases, and which are neither.

See ALSO ...
- *Introducing Elements, Vol. 1: pp. 16–23.*
- *Metals and Metalloids, Vol. 6: pp. 1–65.*
- *Nonmetals, Vol. 7: pp. 1–65.*

▼ *Uranium is one of the rare-earth elements. It is sometimes added to glass to give it a luminous yellow color.*

Chemistry in Action

Rare-earth metals

In most versions of the periodic table, two rows of 14 elements can be found at the bottom of the table. The 14 elements in the first row are called the lanthanide elements, and those in the second row are called the actinide elements. The reason for the separation is a practical one. A period with the full complement of 32 elements is simply too long to fit on a normal page. However, most chemists agree that the chemistry of the lanthanides and actinides is similar enough for the elements to form a separate group, called the rare-earth metals.

5 The Metals

About three-quarters of all the elements are metals. In general, metals are found on the left and in the middle of the periodic table. Some metals, such as gold and copper, were among the first elements to have been discovered.

In nature most metals are found mixed with other elements in rocks, forming compounds called ores. The ores of the metals are usually compounds of oxygen (oxides) or sulfur (sulfides). A few metals, such as gold, platinum, and silver, occur naturally as pure metals.

Metals such as aluminum, copper, iron, and magnesium have many properties such as hardness and strength that make them useful elements. As a result, many metal ores are mined. The metals are then extracted from their ores in a process called refining.

Cog wheels in mechanical devices are commonly made of metals. Many metals are hard and strong, making them ideal for objects that need to withstand a lot of wear and tear.

PLACE ON THE TABLE

Different metals are found in different parts of the table. The alkali metals (Group 1) and alkaline-earth metals (Group 2) can be found on the left side of the table. The transition metals (groups 3–12) are located in the middle of the table. Aluminum (Group 13) and lead and tin (Group 14) are found toward the right side of the table. The rare-earth metals form two rows underneath the main body of the table. The rare-earth metals are considered in chapter 8 of this book.

PHYSICAL PROPERTIES

There are so many different metals that it is hard to talk about general properties. Most metals are hard, dense, and strong solids at room temperature. Mercury is the only metal that is liquid at room temperature (see box on p. 41). Some metals, such as sodium and lithium, are also soft at room temperature and can be cut with a knife. Most metals are silver or gray, but copper is brownish orange and gold is yellow. The surface of a metal shines (has a luster) when it is polished. Most but not all metals have high melting points. The melting point is the temperature at which a solid turns into a liquid. Tungsten has the highest melting point of all the metals—6,192 degrees Fahrenheit (3,422°C). Gallium, however, melts if you hold a piece in your hands. Most metals also have high boiling points. The boiling point is the temperature at which a liquid turns into a gas.

Metals are malleable, which means they can be beaten into different shapes. One ounce (28 g) of gold can be beaten into a sheet 100 feet square (9.3 m²). Metals are also ductile, which means they can be drawn into fine wires. A thread drawn from 1 ton (0.907 metric ton) of gold would stretch to the Moon and back. Most metals are also elastic substances. You can stretch and bend a piece of metal and it will return to its original shape. Metals are also good conductors of heat and electricity.

▼ The metals form the largest group in the periodic table. They are broadly divided into transition metals (Groups 3–12), alkali metals (Group 1), and alkaline-earth metals (Group 2). There are also some metals that fall into Groups 13, 14, 15, and 16.

Group 1 Group 2

Transition metals (Groups 3–12)

Group 13

Group 14

Group 15 Group 16

3 Li Lithium 7	4 Be Beryllium 9												13 Al Aluminum 27			
11 Na Sodium 23	12 Mg Magnesium 24															
19 K Potassium 39	20 Ca Calcium 40	21 Sc Scandium 45	22 Ti Titanium 48	23 V Vanadium 51	24 Cr Chromium 52	25 Mn Manganese 55	26 Fe Iron 56	27 Co Cobalt 59	28 Ni Nickel 59	29 Cu Copper 64	30 Zn Zinc 65	31 Ga Gallium 70			
37 Rb Rubidium 85	38 Sr Strontium 88	39 Y Yttrium 89	40 Zr Zirconium 91	41 Nb Niobium 93	42 Mo Molybdenum 96	43 Tc Technetium (98)	44 Ru Ruthenium 101	45 Rh Rhodium 103	46 Pd Palladium 106	47 Ag Silver 108	48 Cd Cadmium 112	49 In Indium 115	50 Sn Tin 119		
55 Cs Cesium 133	56 Ba Barium 137		72 Hf Hafnium 179	73 Ta Tantalum 181	74 W Tungsten 184	75 Re Rhenium 186	76 Os Osmium 190	77 Ir Iridium 192	78 Pt Platinum 195	79 Au Gold 197	80 Hg Mercury 201	81 Tl Thallium 204	82 Pb Lead 207	83 Bi Bismuth 209	84 Po Polonium (209)
87 Fr Francium 225	88 Ra Radium 226		104 Rf Rutherfordium (263)	105 Db Dubnium (268)	106 Sg Seaborgium (266)	107 Bh Bohrium (272)	108 Hs Hassium (277)	109 Mt Meitnerium (276)	110 Ds Darmstadtium (281)	111 Rg Roentgenium (280)	112 Uub Ununbium (285)	113 Uut Ununtrium (284)	114 Uuq Ununquadium (289)	115 Uup Ununpentium (288)	116 Uuh Ununhexium (292)

THE STRUCTURE OF METALS

Metals are crystalline structures. A solid piece of metal is a huge network of neatly arranged atoms in the form of crystals. This is called a giant lattice structure. The atoms of the metal pack tightly to form the crystals, which are shaped like cubes or hexagons. The bonds holding the atoms together are rigid, making the metal very strong. The tight packing of the atoms makes most metals heavy and dense. Density is a measure of the mass of a substance per unit volume. Osmium and iridium have the highest densities of all the elements.

Sometimes there are defects in the crystal structure. When there is a defect, the atoms in the crystals slide over each other. This makes the metal easy to

▲ This craftsman is applying gold leaf to a table top as a decorative coating. Sheets of gold leaf are only 4–5 millionths of an inch (10–12.4 millionths of a centimeter) thick.

A Closer LOOK

Crystal lattices

In a face-centered cubic lattice, the atoms form a cube with a single atom in the center of each face.

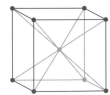

In a body-centered cubic lattice, the atoms form a cube with a single atom at the center of the cube.

In a hexagonal lattice, the atoms form the shape of a hexagon.

◄ Metal crystals are made of atoms arranged in a lattice. The atoms may be arranged in one of three ways, depending on the metal. These arrangements are called hexagonal, face-centered cubic, and body-centered cubic.

stretch and bend and easy to beat into different shapes. That explains why most metals are ductile and malleable. However, too many defects in the crystal make the metal brittle.

In the atoms of most metals, the electrons in the outer electron shell (see pp. 6–7) are not held tightly within the atom. Some of the electrons break free and move among the metal atoms. A metal is therefore a mass of positive ions—metal atoms that have lost electrons. The metal ions are surrounded by a "sea" of electrons. Dutch physicist Hendrik Lorentz (1853–1928) came up with this model of the structure of metals in the early 20th century. It explains why most metals are good conductors. Electricity flows when all the electrons in the sea move in a particular direction.

CHEMICAL PROPERTIES

The atoms of most metals readily give up their outer electrons to the atoms of other elements. Metals therefore form positive ions when they react with other elements, typically nonmetals. The nonmetal atoms accept the electrons and become negative ions. Some metals

A Closer LOOK

Reactivity series

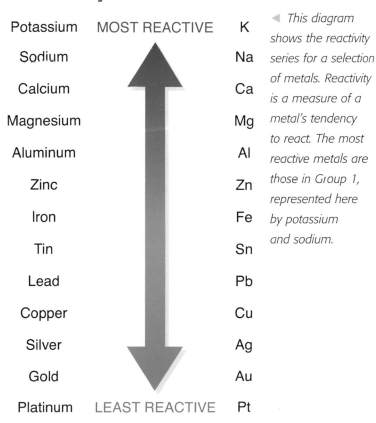

Potassium	MOST REACTIVE	K
Sodium		Na
Calcium		Ca
Magnesium		Mg
Aluminum		Al
Zinc		Zn
Iron		Fe
Tin		Sn
Lead		Pb
Copper		Cu
Silver		Ag
Gold		Au
Platinum	LEAST REACTIVE	Pt

◄ *This diagram shows the reactivity series for a selection of metals. Reactivity is a measure of a metal's tendency to react. The most reactive metals are those in Group 1, represented here by potassium and sodium.*

are much more reactive than others. Potassium and sodium are highly reactive metals. These metals react strongly with water and violently with acids. In both cases, the reaction produces a lot of hydrogen gas and heat. However, gold and silver hardly react at all, even when concentrated (strong) acids are poured on them.

The reactivity series is a list of metals in order of their reactivity. Metals at the top of the series are the most reactive. So the Group 1 metals are found at the top of the reactivity series, and metals such as gold and silver are found at the bottom of the table.

THE ALKALI METALS

The alkali metals form Group 1 of the periodic table. They are lithium, sodium, potassium, rubidium, cesium, and francium. The alkali metals are not very dense. Sodium and potassium are soft enough to be cut with a knife. All the alkali metals have just one electron in their outer electron shell. When they react with other elements, alkali metals

lose this outer electron. The metal becomes a positive ion with a stable arrangement of electrons. The alkali metals therefore form ionic compounds with other elements, particularly the halogens. The alkali metals are the most reactive of all the metals. Common compounds of alkali metals include sodium chloride (table salt) and potassium chloride (a fertilizer).

THE ALKALINE-EARTH METALS

The alkaline earths form Group 2 of the periodic table. They are beryllium, magnesium, calcium, strontium, barium, and radium. Like the alkali metals, the alkaline earths are not as hard or as

Chemistry in Action

Metals in the body

Some metals are vital to body processes. For example, a substance called hemoglobin in the blood contains iron. Hemoglobin enables the blood to carry oxygen from the lungs around the body. Calcium and potassium are needed to transmit signals along nerve cells. Calcium also makes bones and teeth strong and hard. Magnesium plays a role in controlling heartbeat and the functioning of muscles.

▶ A piece of magnesium ribbon burns with a brilliant white light in air. Magnesium is used in flares, aircraft parts, and fireworks.

dense as most other metals. Alkaline-earth metals have two electrons in their outer electron shell. Like the alkali metals, the alkaline earths form ionic compounds with other elements. These metals donate their two outer electrons, forming ions with an electrical charge of +2. The ions formed have an extremely stable arrangement of electrons.

Calcium is the most abundant of the alkaline-earth metals and is the fifth most abundant element in Earth's crust. It is important in the formation of teeth and bones. Compounds of calcium are used in the manufacture of iron and steel.

Strontium-90 is a type of strontium that is radioactive—it breaks down and in the process emits radiation. Strontium-90 is a by-product of reactions that occur in nuclear power stations and can be a very dangerous pollutant. It has a similar chemistry to calcium and so can take the place of calcium in bones. The radiation can cause damage to blood cells and may even cause death.

TRANSITION METALS
The transition metals make up groups 3 through 12 of the periodic table. They include copper, iron, nickel, and zinc. Typically, transition metals are hard, with high melting points.

The chemistry of the transition metals is complex. Many lose one

▼ *This Bronze Age axe head was discovered in France and dates from 2000–500 B.C.E. Bronze is a strong alloy and was useful for making tools and weapons.*

History

The metals of antiquity
Until the end of the 13th century, only seven metals were known—gold, copper, lead, silver, mercury, iron, and tin. These are called the metals of antiquity. Gold was the first of these metals to be discovered and has been in use since around 6000 B.C.E. For much of its history, gold has been used for decorative purposes, such as jewelry and ornaments, though it also now used in electronic devices because it is a good conductor of electricity. Copper was in use by around 4200 B.C.E. and was used for tools and weapons. Silver was first used around 4000 B.C.E. and, like gold, was employed for decorative purposes. Around 3500 B.C.E., Romans were using lead for plumbing and around the same time in the Middle East tin was being added to copper to make the alloy bronze. Alloys are materials made from two or more metals or a metal and a nonmetal. In the case of copper and tin, the resulting alloy is stronger than copper or tin alone. Iron smelting became a common process around 1200 B.C.E., though iron was known about long before this. In the ancient world, iron had many uses, such as weapons and farming implements. Mercury, also known as quicksilver, has been found in an Egyptian tomb of around 1500 B.C.E. It was used to form alloys with gold and silver.

▲ *The silvery metal on this truck is a plating of chromium. Chromium is a transition metal that is used as a plating to give a hard, shiny, and rust-resistant finish.*

TRY THIS

Copper cleaner

Put some copper coins in a bowl containing some vinegar mixed with a teaspoon of table salt. After a few minutes, remove the coins from the salt and vinegar solution. What can you see? Copper coins gradually get dull over time. The copper in the coins reacts with oxygen in the air to form a layer of copper oxide over the surface of the coin. Pure copper is a bright, shiny metal, but copper oxide is dull and green. Vinegar contains a substance called acetic acid. The acid dissolves the copper oxide layer to reveal the shiny copper underneath.

or more electrons from their outer electron shell when they react with other elements. Copper, for example, may lose one electron to form an ion with a single positive charge, or it may lose two electrons to form an ion with a positive charge of two.

Some transition metals have characteristic colors when they form compounds, such as the bright blue crystals of copper sulfate. Many are good electrical conductors because the electrons in the outer electron shell are not bound tightly to each atom. These electrons are therefore free to conduct electricity. Silver is the best conductor of all the metals.

Many transition metals have important uses. Iron is the most widely used and perhaps the most important transition metal. Iron has been used for thousands of years to make tools and weapons. Today, almost all iron is made into an alloy called steel, which contains a mixture of iron with the nonmetal carbon. Steel is used to make buildings, automobiles, ships, bridges, and many other things.

Copper is also very important. Since it is such a good conductor, copper is used to make electrical cables and wires. It is also used to make pipes for water supplies in homes. Some copper is mixed with zinc to make an alloy called brass. Brass is a hard, yellow, shiny alloy commonly used to make decorative items.

OTHER METALS

Aluminum in Group 13 is the most abundant metal in Earth's crust. Like other Group 13 metals, aluminum may donate up to three electrons to other elements when forming compounds. Aluminum is made into food containers, drink cans, kitchen foil, saucepans, and many other objects. It is also a constituent of many alloys.

Group 14 contains two important metals—tin and lead. Both metals are used to make alloys. Bronze is an alloy of copper and tin. People made bronze tools and weapons thousands of years ago. Lead is an important ingredient of the alloys pewter and solder. Pewter is

Key Terms

- **Alkali metals:** Those metals that form Group 1 of the periodic table.
- **Alkaline-earth metals:** Those metals that form Group 2 of the periodic table.
- **Alloys:** Alloys are made of a metal combined with one or more other metals or nonmetals such as carbon.
- **Radioactive element:** An element that breaks down and emits radiation in the process.
- **Transition metals:** Those metals that make up Groups 3 through 12 of the periodic table.

Chemistry in Action

Unusual mercury

Mercury has been known for thousands of years. Early chemists, called alchemists, valued the dense liquid for its unusual properties. Early physicians used mercury as an antiseptic. An antiseptic is a substance that kills or restricts the growth of harmful germs. Since mercury expands evenly when heated, mercury is used in barometers and thermometers, though the use of mercury in thermometers is becoming increasingly rare owing to health concerns. Although the metal is highly poisonous, mercury compounds are still valued for their antiseptic properties. Alloys made with mercury are called amalgams. Amalgams containing various compositions of mercury, zinc, tin, and copper are used in filling teeth.

▲ The Mad Hatter is a character in Lewis Carroll's Alice's Adventures in Wonderland (1865). In real life, hat makers often suffered from mental disorders owing to the poisonous effects of the mercury they used for making felt for hats; hence the phrase "mad as a hatter."

Chemistry in **Action**

Alloys

Steel consists of small amounts of carbon added to iron. Alloys are made of a metal combined with one or more other metals or nonmetals. These combinations can produce materials that have different qualities to their constituent materials. Brass is an alloy of copper and zinc that is more malleable than either of these two elements. It also has good acoustic properties that make it ideal for musical instruments such as trumpets and tubas. Iron on its own is strong but brittle. Adding carbon makes it flexible. Some materials need to have properties that metals alone do not provide. For example, aircraft need to be made of alloys that withstand stresses at high temperatures. Such alloys may contain more than ten different elements to achieve the desired results.

▲ Modern aircraft are made of many alloys. One of the most common metals used to make aircraft alloys is aluminum, which is light but strong.

water pipes but lead is poisonous and many people suffered from lead poisoning as a consequence of this use. Lead is commonly used to make batteries and is a constituent of many types of glass, such as that used to make a type of fine glassware called lead crystal.

Bismuth is the only metal in Group 15. This pinkish metal is a poor conductor of electricity. Many chemists question whether bismuth is a metal or a metalloid. Polonium is a radioactive metal in Group 16. It is only found in tiny amounts in nature.

See ALSO ...
• Metals and Metalloids, Vol. 6: pp. 1–65.

mainly a decorative alloy. Solder is commonly made of tin and lead. Increasingly, however, lead is being replaced in solder with other metals owing to safety issues concerning the use of lead. Lead was once used to make

History

Aluminum

Aluminum was discovered in 1807 by the English scientist Humphry Davy (1778–1829). He was not, however, able to isolate a sample. This did not occur until 1825 when the Danish scientist Hans Christian Oersted (1777–1851) managed to produce minute quantities of this element. By the 1850s techniques for producing more aluminum had been devised but they were still very inefficient. Consequently aluminum at this time was more expensive than gold. So precious was aluminum, that Napoleon III, Emperor of France, even used aluminum cutlery at state banquets. In 1886 a method was finally discovered for producing large quantities of aluminum: the Hall-Héroult process. If a powerful electric current is passed through a bath of a molten mineral called cryolite into which aluminum oxide has been dissolved, then molten aluminum settles at the bottom of the bath. This process was discovered independently by French metallurgist Paul Louis Toussaint Héroult (1863–1914) and U.S. chemist Charles Martin Hall (1863–1914). This method enabled the cheap production of aluminum and is the method by which most aluminum is produced today.

▲ This metal object is called a die. Aluminum is heated until it becomes soft and is then forced through the gaps in the die. This process forms the long upright parts of a ladder, such as that on the left.

6 Nonmetals

The nonmetal elements are Group 17 (the halogens), Group 18 (noble gases), and the following elements, in ascending atomic number: hydrogen, carbon, nitrogen, oxygen, phosphorus, sulfur, and selenium.

There are far fewer nonmetal elements than metal elements in the periodic table. However, the nonmetals far outweigh the metals in terms of abundance on Earth. Earth's atmosphere consists entirely of nonmetals, mostly nitrogen and oxygen, with tiny amounts of other gases. Oxygen, in combination with other elements, also makes up nearly half of Earth's crust. The nonmetals, particularly carbon, are vital for all living organisms to enable them to live, breathe, and grow. Without the nonmetals humans could not exist.

Nonmetals are everywhere. They make up the rocks on the seabed, the water of the oceans, the oxygen in the divers' tanks, the bubbles of carbon dioxide rising to the surface, and most of the body of the divers.

					2 **He** Helium 4
1 **H** Hydrogen 1	6 **C** Carbon 12	7 **N** Nitrogen 14	8 **O** Oxygen 16	9 **F** Fluorine 19	10 **Ne** Neon 20
	15 **P** Phosphorus 31	16 **S** Sulfur 32	17 **Cl** Chlorine 35	18 **Ar** Argon 40	
		34 **Se** Selenium 79	35 **Br** Bromine 80	36 **Kr** Krypton 84	
			53 **I** Iodine 127	54 **Xe** Xenon 131	
			85 **At** Astatine (210)	84 **Rn** Radon (222)	

PHYSICAL PROPERTIES

The nonmetals show a range of physical properties. At normal temperatures and pressures, most nonmetals are gases, a few are solids, and bromine is a liquid. Unlike metals, most nonmetals do not conduct heat and electricity very well. Their melting points are generally lower than those of metals. Solid nonmetals are also brittle and lack the characteristic shiny surfaces of metals.

CHEMICAL PROPERTIES

Almost all nonmetals consist of small atoms with many electrons in their outer electron shell. The outer electron shell of the noble gases is full. As a result, the atoms of the noble gases are stable. They do not readily give up or share their electrons with the atoms of other elements. The outer electron shell of other nonmetal atoms is at least half full or nearly full. In most cases nonmetals form compounds by accepting electrons or sharing electrons with other atoms. Adding or sharing electrons results in a full outer shell, which is more stable than a partially full outer shell. Nonmetals often accept electrons from metal atoms to form strongly bonded ionic compounds. With other nonmetals they form bonds by sharing electrons (covalent bonds).

HYDROGEN

Hydrogen is the most common element in the universe. It is unique among the nonmetals. The atoms of this invisible, odorless gas are relatively small. Each

▲ The nonmetals make up the upper right-hand portion of the table. Most of them are gases, but some are solids. Hydrogen, which is usually placed on the left of the table in Group 1, is included with these elements because it is a gas.

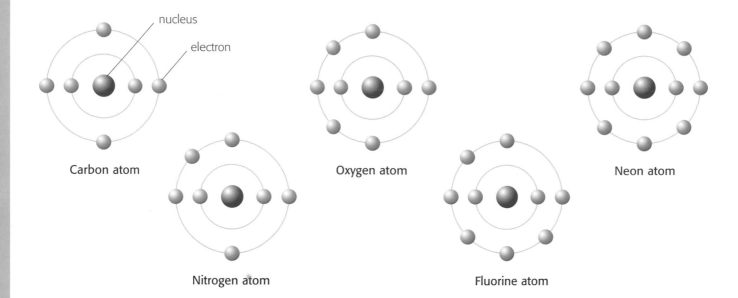

nucleus

electron

Carbon atom

Nitrogen atom

Oxygen atom

Fluorine atom

Neon atom

▲ *The outer electron shell of nonmetals ranges from half full (carbon) to completely full (neon). Nonmetals form a wide range of compounds by sharing electrons with other nonmetals or gaining electrons from other elements. Only neon, which has a full outer shell, does not react chemically.*

one has just one electron in its outer electron shell. The hydrogen atom tends to donate this electron to the atoms of other elements during chemical reactions. In this way, it reacts more like a metal than a nonmetal. For this reason, hydrogen is usually placed above the Group 1 metals on the left of the periodic table. Like many gaseous nonmetals, hydrogen is found as diatomic molecules (two atoms linked by a single bond) in nature (see p. 50). Natural gas is the main source of hydrogen on Earth.

Hydrogen is very explosive. The gas was once used to lift giant airships in the early 20th century. However, so many disasters occurred that all the hydrogen-inflated airships were taken out of service. Today, hydrogen is used to make a range of

important chemicals, such as ammonia and acids, and has applications in the manufacture of margarine and as a fuel.

NONMETAL SOLIDS
Three nonmetals are solids at normal conditions. They are carbon (Group 14), phosphorus (Group 15), and sulfur (Group 16). All three elements exist in different structural forms, called

▼ *Hydrogen is the lightest element, capable of supporting airships, but it is also highly flammable. In 1937 the German airship* Hindenburg *exploded, killing 36 people. Helium proved much safer.*

allotropes. A substance is said to be an allotrope when two or more different forms occur in the same state, whether solid, liquid, or gas.

Carbon has several solid allotropes including graphite and diamond. Each allotrope consists of a regular arrangement of carbon atoms. In diamond this crystal structure is extremely stable. As a result, diamond is one of the hardest substances known in nature. Diamonds are therefore useful in cutting tools. They are also highly prized as gemstones.

By contrast the crystals of graphite form layers that move over one another easily. Graphite is sometimes used as a lubricant thanks to the sliding properties of its crystals. Graphite is also mixed

▶ *The most expensive allotropes in the world are the sparkling cut-diamond form of carbon.*

Chemistry in Action

Organic chemistry

Carbon atoms can form bonds with many other carbon atoms. When other elements join with the carbon atoms, an almost endless variety of compounds can form. For example, hydrocarbons are compounds of carbon and hydrogen. Hydrocarbons form the basis of billion-dollar chemical industries, from paint to petroleum. More complex carbon compounds, such as carbohydrates and proteins, are the foundations for every living organism. Indeed, carbon makes up about 20 percent of the weight of the human body. The study of these carbon compounds is called organic chemistry (*see* vol. 8). It is one of the largest and most important branches of chemistry.

◀ *Matches contain two nonmetal elements— sulfur and phosphorus. The sulfur is in the match head. The phosphorus is coated along the side of the box. Striking the match energizes the phosphorus and ignites the sulfur and other chemicals in the head.*

▼ *Plants such as these (uprooted) peanuts need phosphorus and nitrogen to grow. Peanuts have nodules on their roots where bacteria live that can convert nitrogen into a usable form.*

with clay and used as the "lead" in pencils. It is also the only nonmetallic element that conducts electricity.

The two most important phosphorus allotropes are the white and red forms. An allotrope called black phosphorus exists, but it can only be made under high pressure. Similar to carbon, phosphorus allotropes differ in their crystal structure. White phosphorus is the most reactive allotrope. This waxy solid is stored under oil or water to prevent it from reacting with oxygen in the air. White phosphorus is used to create smoke screens during military operations. Red phosphorus is much more stable than white phosphorus. It is used to make safety matches and fireworks. Like carbon, phosphorus is an important element in living organisms,

particularly as the phosphates in bones and teeth, and also in the process of photosynthesis in plants. Photosynthesis is the process by which plants convert carbon dioxide and water into food.

Sulfur is the ninth most abundant element on Earth. It is often found

Chemistry in Action

Stinky sulfur

While pure sulfur is odorless, this element has a tendency to form some extremely smelly compounds. The gas hydrogen sulfide (H_2S) is perhaps the most familiar, with its smell of rotten eggs. This smell is often encountered in wells or water systems contaminated with bacteria that produce hydrogen sulfide. It is also released from oil wells, volcanoes, and some thermal springs. Hydrogen sulfide is perhaps better known to many schoolchildren as the main ingredient in stink bombs.

Sulfur also occurs in many organic compounds, especially substances called thiols, or mercaptans. Thiols are responsible for the smells of garlic, boiled cabbage, bad breath, and rotting flesh. Thiols are also used to great effect by animals such as skunks, which spray thiols to warn off predators. However, thiols can be useful—gas companies add a tiny amount to odorless natural gas so that people can detect a gas leak. Not all thiols smell bad. Some of the aromas in wine and the smell of grapefruits are also produced by thiols.

combined with useful metals in the form of ores. Underground deposits of pure sulfur are also common around hot springs and volcanoes.

Elemental sulfur (sulfur in its pure, uncombined state) usually occurs as pale yellow crystals. However, chemists have identified up to eight different allotropes. Sulfur is an extremely important element in the chemical industry. Most is used to make sulfuric acid. Other uses include the manufacture of detergents, rubber, explosives, petroleum, and many other essential products.

NITROGEN AND OXYGEN

Nitrogen and oxygen are the two main gases in Earth's atmosphere. About 78 percent of the volume of the atmosphere is nitrogen and 21 percent is oxygen. Most of the nitrogen and oxygen used in the chemical industry is taken from the air. At room temperature, nitrogen is a colorless, odorless, unreactive gas because of its tendency to form diatomic molecules (*see* p. 50). It has many applications, ranging from the manufacture of ammonia and nitric acid to its use in dyes, explosives, and

▲ *Skunks are given a wide berth by anyone who comes into contact with them, especially when a skunk raises its tail to spray. The foul smell of the sulfur-containing spray is so powerful, only a few drops are necessary to deter predators or people.*

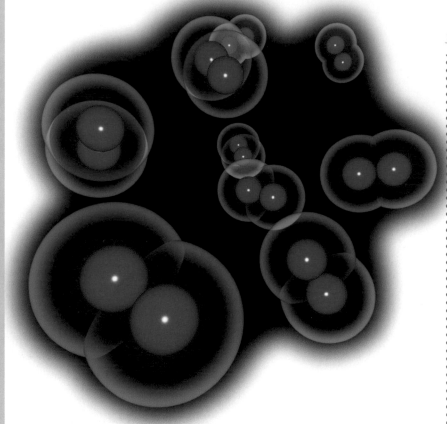

A Closer LOOK

Diatomic molecules

Diatomic molecules are compounds in which two nonmetal atoms, whether the same or different elements, are joined by the attraction of sharing electrons (covalent bonds). In nature, seven nonmetals occur as diatomic elements. These nonmetals are hydrogen (H_2), nitrogen (N_2), oxygen (O_2), fluorine (F_2), chlorine (Cl_2), bromine (Br_2), and iodine (I_2). Earth's atmosphere consists almost entirely (99 percent) of diatomic oxygen and nitrogen. Other examples of diatomic molecules include carbon monoxide (CO), hydrogen fluoride (HF), and nitric oxide (NO).

▲ *This illustration shows diatomic oxygen molecules (O_2). Atmospheric oxygen commonly occurs in this form. Sometimes three atoms join into one molecule. This molecule is called ozone (O_3).*

fertilizers. Liquid nitrogen is used as a refrigerant by many industries and to keep medical samples frozen.

Like many nonmetals, nitrogen is an important part of the chemistry of living organisms. Many molecules in the human body contain nitrogen atoms. Humans obtain nitrogen by eating plants, which in turn extract it from the soil. One way that nitrogen enters the soil is during thunderstorms, when lightning forces nitrogen and oxygen atoms in the air to react and form nitrogen oxides, which are then washed into the soil by rain. Soil bacteria can also convert atmospheric nitrogen into compounds called nitrates. The nitrates are then taken up by plants.

In nature, both nitrogen and oxygen are usually found as diatomic molecules (*see* box above). Oxygen also exists as the molecule ozone (O_3), which is a combination of three oxygen atoms. Like nitrogen, oxygen is an invisible, odorless gas. Many substances react with oxygen in the air when they are left out in the open. Burning simply involves heating a substance in the air. The substance then reacts with the oxygen in the air.

Oxygen is stored as a liquid and mainly used in the steelmaking industry. Liquid oxygen is also used as a rocket fuel. Naturally, oxygen is vital to animals since they need it to breathe. Plants produce oxygen during a process called photosynthesis (*see* vol. 9: pp. 41–43).

THE HALOGENS

The halogens form Group 17 of the periodic table. At room temperature, the physical properties of the halogens vary from solid iodine, through liquid bromine, to the gases fluorine and chlorine. The chemical properties are typical of nonmetals. The halogens usually take in an electron from the atoms of other elements. They are highly

History

▲ Carl Scheele was the first to find that heating oxides gave off a gas.

▲ Antoine Lavoisier made the key connection between oxygen and burning.

▲ Joseph Priestley's work provided the basis for Lavoisier's experiments.

Who discovered oxygen?

In the early 1770s, scientists were trying to understand the chemistry of combustion (burning). Many thought that matter contained a substance called phlogiston. As substances burned, phlogiston was thought to pour into the air. The phlogiston theory was also used to explain how animals breathed and metals rusted. In 1772, Swedish chemist Carl Wilhelm Scheele (1742–1786) experimented with combustion by heating metal oxides and noted that an invisible gas was given off. Two years later, English chemist Joseph Priestley (1733–1804) also made the same discovery. Neither Priestley nor Scheele realized how close they were to the truth. This was left to French chemist Antoine-Laurent Lavoisier (1743–1794). Lavoisier was also doing experiments in combustion in Paris, France. He was convinced that the phlogiston theory was wrong. When he heard about Priestley's experiments, Lavoisier realized that the invisible gas was responsible for combustion. Lavoisier noted that the gas formed acidic compounds with many substances. He named it *oxygine*, from the Greek words meaning "acid former." Lavoisier took all the credit for himself. The role of Scheele and Priestley was ignored for many years.

Chemistry in Action

Selenium

Selenium is the third nonmetal in Group 16 of the periodic table. In nature selenium is almost always found mixed with sulfur and metals such as copper and lead. As a pure element, selenium exists in one of many different forms, called allotropes. In some cases, selenium occurs as a red powder or black, glassy solid. Selenium can also exist as red crystals. The most common allotrope looks like a gray, metallic solid. Due to its metal-like appearance, some chemists think that the element is a metalloid. Metalloids have properties similar to both metals and nonmetals in different circumstances (*see* pp. 54–59).

▲ *Swimming pools often use chlorine or chlorine dioxide as a disinfectant to kill any germs that may be lurking in the water.*

reactive, and fluorine is the most reactive element of all. For example, the halogens readily react with the alkali metals to form ionic compounds. The atom of the alkali metal donates one electron to the atom of the halogen, resulting in a stable ionic compound. Common salt (sodium chloride) is perhaps the most familiar example. Its chemical formula is $NaCl$.

The halogens have many different uses. Chlorine is sometimes added to swimming pools to kill harmful germs in the water. Fluorine is often found in toothpastes and drinking water because it is thought to help strengthen the teeth and bones. Iodine is a dark-purple solid, and is an essential nutrient in the human diet. It is also often used as a mild antiseptic, helping to kill or restrict the growth of harmful germs on the skin.

NOBLE GASES

The noble gases form Group 18 (sometimes called Group 0) of the periodic table. All of this group are gases at normal room temperature, and they all have low boiling points. The outer electron shell of each noble gas is full. The atoms are stable and do not normally react with the atoms of other elements.

The noble gases used to be called the "inert" gases. The word *inert* means "totally unreactive." This implies that the gases do not react with any other substances. In laboratory conditions, however, xenon has been made to react with fluorine. The word *noble* is now the accepted term for gases in Group 18. In chemistry and alchemy, the word *noble* has also been used to describe metals that do not react with oxygen.

The noble gases have a number of important uses. Helium is an invisible, odorless gas. Since it is unreactive and much lighter than air and safer than hydrogen, it is an ideal gas for inflating hot-air balloons and airships. Scientists are also interested in liquid helium because it has some strange and unusual properties. It does not boil and cannot be made solid by reducing the temperature. At very low temperatures it can even defy gravity and creep up and over the walls of its container.

Neon lighting is another valuable application of the noble gases. Neon is usually used to make brightly colored lights, but xenon and krypton lights are also popular. Xenon also fills the flashtubes of stroboscopic (flashing on and off) equipment. Photography flashlights are increasingly filled with krypton. Argon is often used to prevent metals from oxidizing during welding.

▼ *Lightbulbs are filled with gases that glow when they are switched on. Many of these gases are noble gases, such as neon, krypton, or xenon. Halogens are also used in many types of lights, such as in car headlights and fog lamps, where they give a brilliant white light.*

See ALSO ...
- Introducing Elements, Vol. 1: pp. 16–23.
- Nonmetals, Vol. 7: pp. 1–65.
- Chemistry in Industry, Vol. 10: pp. 4–21.

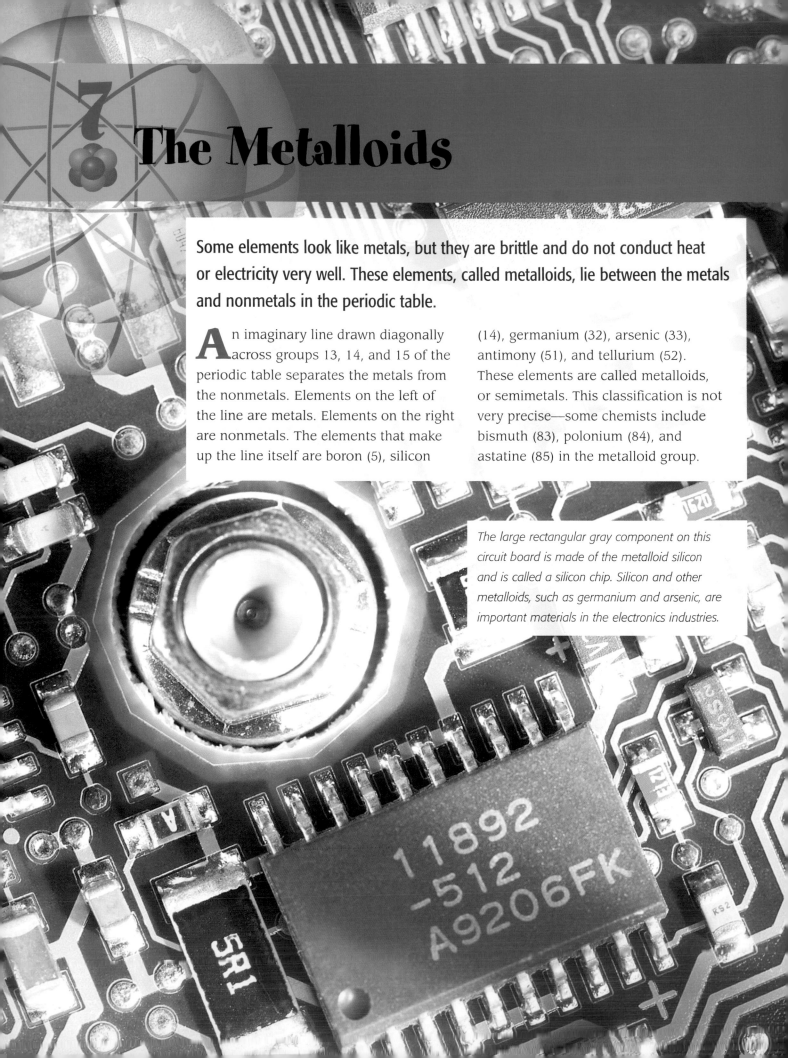

7 The Metalloids

Some elements look like metals, but they are brittle and do not conduct heat or electricity very well. These elements, called metalloids, lie between the metals and nonmetals in the periodic table.

An imaginary line drawn diagonally across groups 13, 14, and 15 of the periodic table separates the metals from the nonmetals. Elements on the left of the line are metals. Elements on the right are nonmetals. The elements that make up the line itself are boron (5), silicon (14), germanium (32), arsenic (33), antimony (51), and tellurium (52). These elements are called metalloids, or semimetals. This classification is not very precise—some chemists include bismuth (83), polonium (84), and astatine (85) in the metalloid group.

The large rectangular gray component on this circuit board is made of the metalloid silicon and is called a silicon chip. Silicon and other metalloids, such as germanium and arsenic, are important materials in the electronics industries.

GENERAL PROPERTIES

Metalloids have some of the properties of metals and some of nonmetals. As a result, they show a wide range of properties. For example, the surface of a piece of arsenic is shiny like a metal. Unlike most metals, however, arsenic is a rather weak solid—arsenic is brittle and a chunk of arsenic breaks easily. True metals rarely form compounds with other metals. Arsenic readily forms compounds with metals. Arsenopyrite, for example, is a compound made of iron, arsenic, and sulfur and has the chemical formula FeAsS. Arsenopyrite is the most common naturally occurring mineral that contains arsenic.

Some metalloids act both as electrical conductors and insulators. In some circumstances, they will conduct electricity and in others they will not. Substances that behave in this way are called semiconductors. Boron, germanium, and silicon are the most important semiconductors.

BORON

Boron is the first element in Group 13 of the periodic table. Credit for its discovery usually goes to French chemists Joseph-Louis Gay-Lussac (1778–1850) and Louis-Jacques Thénard (1777–1857) in 1808. English chemist Humphry Davy (1778–1829) also made the discovery independently in the same year. Boron is a black, brittle, shiny solid. It is extremely hard, and for this reason it may be added to steel and other alloys to make them even harder. Boron and its compounds have many other uses. Boric acid, or borax, is an important compound of boron. Borax is a mild antiseptic that stops harmful germs from growing on the skin. Borax is also widely used in industry, for example, in leather tanning and glassmaking. Boron is also an essential trace element for plants.

GERMANIUM

The discovery of germanium (Group 14) is an important event in the history of the periodic table. When Mendeleyev drew up his 1869 table in order of atomic mass, he left some gaps in it. He suggested that the gaps would be

▼ The metalloids (blue) form a diagonal across the periodic table and divide the metals (orange) from the nonmetals (green).

5 **B** Boron 11	6 C Carbon 12	7 N Nitrogen 14	8 O Oxygen 16
13 Al Aluminum 27	14 **Si** Silicon 28	15 P Phosphorus 31	16 S Sulfur 32
31 Ga Gallium 70	32 **Ge** Germanium 73	33 **As** Arsenic 75	34 Se Selenium 79
49 In Indium 115	50 Sn Tin 119	51 **Sb** Antimony 122	52 **Te** Tellurium 128

filled by new elements that were unknown to scientists of the time. He also predicted the exact chemical properties of the new elements.

In 1886 German chemist Clemens Winkler (1838–1904) discovered a new element, which he called germanium. The discovery matched Mendeleyev's prediction for one such element, which he had called eka-silicon because it would sit underneath silicon in the periodic table.

Like all the metalloids, germanium is a brittle solid with a shiny surface. Like boron and silicon, it is used as a semiconductor in the electronics industry. It is also used to make glass lenses for cameras and microscopes.

SILICON

Silicon is found underneath carbon in Group 14 of the periodic table. Around 30 percent of the Earth's crust consists of silicon. Pure silicon is a hard, gray solid with a shiny surface. In nature, however, silicon is found combined with oxygen in the form of silicon dioxide (SiO_2), also known as silica. Silica is the most abundant compound in Earth's crust. Silica can take many forms but the most common is quartz. Clay commonly contains silica, and in many places silica is the main component of sand. Sand is made mostly of tiny pieces of quartz and is an important building material. Quartz is heated and shaped to make glass.

▼ *The white islands on this lake in Bolivia are deposits of borax. Borax is a major source of the metalloid boron.*

◀ *Citrine is a form of yellow quartz (silicon dioxide). Quartz can take several different forms such as amethyst (purple) and rose quartz (pink).*

Silicones are another valuable group of silicon products. Lubricants, varnishes, adhesives, cosmetics, and many other goods are made using silicones.

SILICON CHIPS

By far the most important use for silicon is in the semiconductor industry. Silicon is used to make a wide range of electronic parts. Wafer-thin slices of silicon, called silicon chips, are an

Chemistry in Action

Semiconductors

The outer electrons in a metal's atoms are not tightly bound to the nucleus. They can move freely through the metal. This movement of electrons makes up an electrical current, and therefore metals are good conductors. By contrast, the atoms of nonmetals hold on very tightly to their electrons. The electrons cannot move about as freely, and nonmetals are insulators.

Pure silicon is an insulator at low temperatures. The electrons in the silicon atoms are used to form bonds with neighboring silicon atoms. As the temperature rises, however, the electrons break free from the bonds. These electrons can then move through the silicon, and electricity can flow. For this reason, silicon is called a semiconductor.

Silicon can also be made a better conductor by adding small amounts of other substances, such as phosphorus and boron. This process is called doping. Although silicon conducts electricity under the right conditions, it will never conduct electricity as well as a metal.

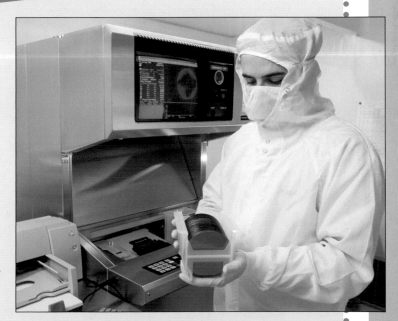

▲ *These circular wafers of silicon are used to make silicon chips. Silicon chips contain thousands of tiny electrical components that take advantage of silicon's properties as a semiconductor.*

History

Metalloid murder

The poisonous effects of arsenic have been known since at least Roman times. Arsenic was often used as a means of murdering people, whether to settle scores or for political reasons. Its great advantages as an instrument of murder are that it is colorless, odorless, and tasteless. Also, the effects of arsenic poisoning are similar to food poisoning. The victim experiences severe abdominal cramps, vomiting, diarrhea and, if the dose is large enough, death from shock. Throughout history there have been many famous poisoners who used arsenic. In Italy, during the Middle Ages, members of the Borgia family were notorious for poisoning their political opponents. In 19th-century England, the serial killer Mary Anne Cotton used arsenic in cups of tea to murder at least 21 people, including three of her husbands and several of her children. In the 1830s, English chemist James Marsh devised a test for arsenic that enabled scientists to detect whether someone had been poisoned using this metalloid. Following this invention, arsenic poisoning as a means of murder fell out of favor.

integral part of computers. The chips contain tiny electrical circuits that control the microprocessor—the computer's brain.

The first computers were enormous machines that filled entire rooms. Impressive as they were at the time, these early computers could perform the same tasks as a handheld calculator can today. Silicon chips have revolutionized electronics. The chips themselves are cut from a single silicon crystal. Millions of tiny components, called transistors, are then etched on the silicon using lasers. The resulting silicon chip can then be used to control an electronic device. The

Key Terms

- **Antiseptic:** A substance that kills or restricts the growth of harmful germs.
- **Conductor:** A substance through which heat or electricity flow easily.
- **Insulator:** A substance that is a poor conductor of heat or electricity.
- **Microprocessor:** A tiny silicon chip that contains all the electronic circuits used to run a computer. The microprocessor is the computer's "brain."
- **Semiconductor:** A substance that conducts heat and electricity but only in certain circumstances.

▲ Arsenic is poisonous and is no longer as freely available as it once was. Today it is used in the electronics industry to make semiconductors. A compound of arsenic, arsenic trioxide, is used to treat leukemia.

History

Tellurium

Tellurium has a special place in the history of the periodic table. Around 1860, French geologist Alexandre-Emile Bèguyer de Chancourtois (1820–1886) arranged the known elements in a spiral around a cylinder. He placed the elements in order of atomic weight. De Chancourtois called his arrangement the "telluric spiral," because tellurium was situated in the center of the spiral. Tellurium is a rare silvery white metalloid with a shiny metal-like surface, but it is also extremely brittle. Tellurium is added to alloys to improve the strength and wear of the alloy.

▶ *A compound of tellurium is used in the solar cells that cover the roof of this gas station. Enough energy is obtained from these solar cells to power the gas pumps and light the station.*

chip is often called an integrated circuit, because it integrates (connects) all the electronics on a single piece of silicon.

ANTIMONY

Antimony is most commonly found in the mineral stibnite. Antimony has been known of in compounds since ancient times, when it was used in cosmetics and medicines. It has been regarded as a metalloid element since at least the 17th century. Antimony and many of its compounds are highly toxic. It has many industrial uses, such as in semiconductors, in alloys that expand when they solidify, and in the manufacture of enamels. It is also used in lead alloys that are used to make lead batteries.

See ALSO ...
● *Metals and Metalloids, Vol. 6: pp. 1–65.*

Rare-earth Metals

The black sand of this beach is made of monazite, a mineral that contains a high proportion of rare-earth elements.

The rare-earth metals form two rows of elements below the main body of the periodic table. The first row contains the lanthanides (lanthanum to lutetium). The second row contains the actinides (actinium to lawrencium).

57 La Lanthanum 39	58 Ce Cerium 140	59 Pr Praseodymium 141	60 Nd Neodymium 144	61 Pm Promethium (145)	62 Sm Samarium 150	63 Eu Europium 152	64 Gd Gadolinium 157	65 Tb Terbium 159	66 Dy Dysprosium 163	67 Ho Holmium 165	68 Er Erbium 167	69 Tm Thulium 169	70 Yb Ytterbium 173	71 Lu Lutetium 175
89 Ac Actinium 227	90 Th Thorium 232	91 Pa Protactinium 231	92 U Uranium 238	93 Np Neptunium (237)	94 Pu Plutonium (244)	95 Am Americium (243)	96 Cm Curium (247)	97 Bk Berkelium (247)	98 Cf Californium (251)	99 Es Einsteinium (252)	100 Fm Fermium (257)	101 Md Mendelevium (258)	102 No Nobelium (259)	103 Lr Lawrencium (260)

The rare-earth metals usually sit as a separate block at the bottom of the periodic table.

Look at the periodic table on pages 24–25 of this book. Follow the elements along Period 6. The period starts with cesium (55), then barium (56). The atomic number (*see* p. 5) then jumps to hafnium (72) and continues in sequence until radon (86) at the end of the row. The same thing happens in Period 7. After francium (87) and radium (88), the atomic number jumps to rutherfordium (104). It then continues until element 116 at the end of the row.

The missing elements lanthanum (57) to lutetium (71) and actinium (89) to lawrencium (103) appear in two separate rows at the bottom of the periodic table. The elements in the first row are called the lanthanide elements. The elements in the second row are called the actinide elements. Together these elements are called the rare-earth metals.

PHYSICAL PROPERTIES

The rare earths share many common properties. For this reason, it is often difficult to tell them apart. All are silvery white to gray solids with shiny surfaces, but they tarnish (discolor) in the air. The discoloration occurs because the metals readily react with oxygen in the air. The oxygen combines with the metal to form a compound called a metal oxide. The thin layer of metal oxide coats the surface of the metal. Like most metals, the rare earths are good conductors of heat and electricity.

In nature, many rare-earth metals occur mixed with other elements to form rocks and minerals. Minerals that contain valuable elements are called ores. Because the rare earths are all so similar in their chemical properties, they often occur together and are difficult to separate. Monazite is an ore of several mixed rare-earth metals and the elements phosphorus and oxygen. The rare-earth metals are often found in combination with nonmetals. Each metal atom gives up three electrons in its outer electron shell to form chemical bonds

with the nonmetal atom. In some cases, the atom may lose just two or four outer electrons, forming compounds with different properties.

THE LANTHANIDE ELEMENTS

The name *rare-earth metal* is slightly misleading for the lanthanide elements. The lanthanides are not as rare as chemists first thought. Some lanthanides are more common than better-known

▲ *This 1930s poster is advertising a face cream that contains thorium, a radioactive rare-earth element. The cream also contains another radioactive element, radium. Both were once thought to be beneficial to health!*

61

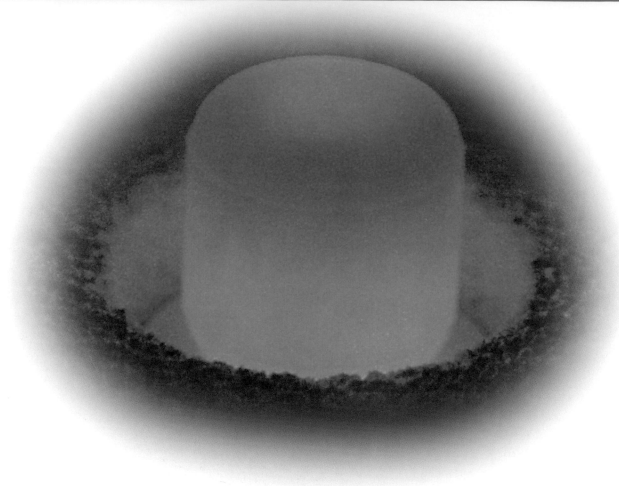

metals such as platinum or lead, for example. Only promethium has to be made artificially.

The lanthanides are relatively soft metals, but their hardness increases as the atomic number increases from left to right across the period. Lanthanides have a high melting and boiling point, and they are extremely reactive. The lanthanides react readily with most nonmetals. Generally, they lose three outer electrons to form bonds with nonmetal atoms. They react with water and weak acids and burn easily in air.

The lanthanides and their compounds have many uses. Some are useful catalysts, speeding up chemical reactions in the petroleum industry. Others are

▲ *This pellet of plutonium glows with radioactivity. Plutonium forms as part of the decay process of uranium. Plutonium is used as a fuel source for space probes and in nuclear power plants. It is highly toxic and dangerous even at very low quantities.*

Key Terms

- **Alloy:** Mixture of two or more metals or a metal and a nonmetal such as carbon.
- **Boiling point:** The temperature at which a liquid turns into a gas.
- **Melting point:** The temperature at which a solid turns into a liquid.
- **Ore:** Mineral that contains useful elements such as aluminum or copper.
- **Radioactivity:** The release of energy that results when the nucleus of an atom breaks down.
- **Transuranium elements:** Elements with an atomic number greater than that of uranium, which is 92.

used to make lasers and fluorescent lamps. They are also used in televisions in the screen coatings that provide colored images. Some lanthanides are mixed with other metals to make alloys. The lanthanide metal adds to the strength of the final alloy. Some rare earths also have magnetic properties that are useful at extremely low temperatures where other magnetic elements do not work.

THE ACTINIDE ELEMENTS

The actinide elements are dense, radioactive metals. Over time, their atoms break down to form the atoms of other elements. Some are very unstable and will only form compounds with elements that increase their stability. Like most metals, the actinides react with weak acids to release hydrogen. This gas is also given off when the actinides are placed in boiling water. The actinides react readily with oxygen in the air, which discolors the metal with a thin layer of metal oxide.

Uranium is the most common element of the actinides and is widely distributed around the world. It usually occurs as an oxide, uranium dioxide, UO_2. As the most abundant radioactive element, uranium is mined and processed for use in the nuclear power industry. Some uranium is also used to make a luminous yellowy green glass. Thorium also occurs in many parts of the world in the mineral monazite and may be even more common than uranium. Thorium is mainly used in the making of mantles for gas lamps, but also has uses as a catalyst in the production of nitric and sulfuric acids and in the oil industry.

Thorium, too, has potential for use as a nuclear fuel. The other actinide elements have limited uses. Plutonium is used to power heart pacemakers and in the nuclear industry. Americium is used in smoke detectors.

BUILDING THE ACTINIDES

Only the first four elements in the actinide series occur in any significant quantity in nature. These are actinium, thorium, protactinium, and uranium. Actinides with an atomic number greater

▼ *Edwin McMillan (1907–1991) was one of the scientists who discovered neptunium, which follows uranium in the actinide series. He shared the Nobel Prize for this discovery with Glenn Seaborg in 1951.*

Profile

Glenn Theodore Seaborg

Glenn Theodore Seaborg was born in Ishpeming, Michigan, on April 19, 1912. When he was a child, the family moved to Los Angeles, California. Seaborg studied at the University of California, Los Angeles (UCLA). He graduated in 1934 with a degree in chemistry. He then did postgraduate studies at the University of California, Berkeley. There, he studied with some of the leading scientists of the day, including American chemist Gilbert Lewis (1875–1946). Seaborg's research continued at Berkeley. Eventually, he became professor of chemistry.

It was during World War II (1939–1945) that Seaborg made his mark on the periodic table. In addition to plutonium, Seaborg discovered the elements americium, curium, berkelium, californium, einsteinium, fermium, mendelevium, and nobelium. In recognition of his contribution to chemistry, Seaborg shared the 1951 Nobel Prize with Edwin McMillian. Seaborg died in 1999, following complications after a stroke. The element seaborgium (106) is named in his honor.

▶ *Professor Glenn Seaborg was one of the most active researchers in the field of actinide elements.*

than 92 (uranium) are known as the transuranium elements. Of these, only neptunium and plutonium have been found in nature, and even then only in trace amounts. All the other transuranium elements are synthetic elements made in the laboratory.

In 1940 American physicists Edwin McMillan (1907–1991) and Philip Abelson (1913–2004) produced an element with the atomic number 93. They named the element neptunium. A year later U.S. chemist Glenn T. Seaborg (1912–1999) and his colleagues produced element 94, named plutonium. In 1944, after more transuranium elements were discovered, Seaborg suggested that these elements should form a group similar to the lanthanide series. He called the new group the actinide series and placed both the lanthanides and actinides in a block at the bottom of the periodic table. Seaborg's revision was the last major change to the layout of the table.

END OF THE PERIODIC TABLE

The search for even heavier elements than seaborgium has continued since the 1970s. Much of the work has been carried out at laboratories in Darmstadt in Germany, Dubna in Russia, and Berkeley in California. Because these elements do not occur naturally they have to be created.

The key to the process of making a new element lies in the ratio of protons and neutrons in the nucleus of an atom. If the ratio is not correct, the nucleus becomes unstable and the atom breaks apart. Certain combinations of protons and neutrons are very stable and are called "magic" numbers. The most stable heavy element in nature is lead, with 82 protons and 126 neutrons. Beyond this ideal ratio, researchers have predicted other combinations of protons and neutrons that could result in new "superheavy" elements. Researchers prepare them by bombarding one heavy element, such as americium or curium, with another rich in neutrons. That starts a fusion reaction that begins a radioactive decay chain (*see* vol.1: pp. 60–61). The presence of the new element is detected by analyzing the products that form. Using this method the elements bohrium (107), hassium (108), meitnerium (109), darmstadtium (110), and roentgenium (111) have been discovered.

Some researchers claim to have detected evidence that elements up to number 118 may have formed during experiments. However, they have not produced enough of the new element to prove this. In some cases as few as one or two atoms have been created.

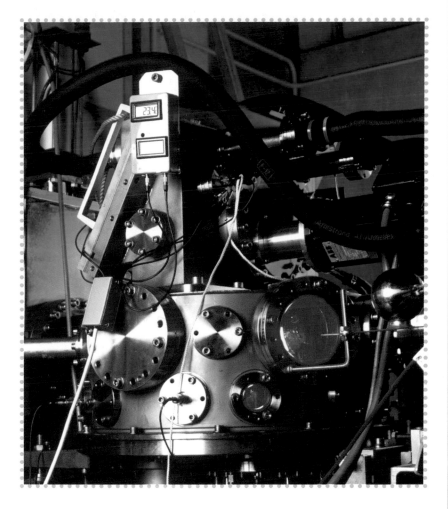

▲ *This equipment at Darmstadt in Germany is used to fuse heavy atoms together to form new elements.*

In theory chemists think that the maximum atomic number possible (the number of protons the nucleus can hold) lies somewhere between 170 and 210. However, it is doubtful whether chemists will actually identify such a large number of elements. The laws of science do not rule out the possibility of 210 protons in an atom, but the stability of the nucleus does. In fact, chemists may be close to finding all the elements of the periodic table. They think the maximum atomic number is about 120, which means there are eight or so new elements left to be discovered.

See Also ...
• *Radioactivity, Vol. 1: pp. 56–65.*
• *Atoms and Elements, Vol. 5: pp. 4–9.*

More Information

BOOKS

Atkins, P. W. *The Periodic Kingdom: A Journey into the Land of Chemical Elements.* New York, NY: Basic Books, 1997.

Bendick, J., and Wiker, B. *The Mystery of the Periodic Table (Living History Library).* Bathgate, ND: Bethlehem Books, 2003.

Berg, J., Stryer, L., and Tymoczko, J. *Biochemistry.* New York, NY: W. H. Freeman, 2002.

Brown, T., Burdge, J., Bursten, B., and LeMay, E. *Chemistry: The Central Science.* 10th ed. Englewood Cliffs, NJ: Prentice Hall, 2005.

Cobb, C., and Fetterolf, M. L. *The Joy of Chemistry: The Amazing Science of Familiar Things.* Amherst, NY: Prometheus Books, 2005.

Cox, M., and Nelson, D. *Lehninger's Principles of Biochemistry.* 4th ed. New York, NY: W. H. Freeman, 2004.

Davis, M. *Modern Chemistry.* New York, NY: Henry Holt, 2000.

Herr, N., and Cunningham, J. *Hands-on Chemistry Activities with Real Life Applications.* Hoboken, NJ: Jossey-Bass, 2002.

Houck, Clifford C., and Post, Richard. *Chemistry: Concepts and Problems.* Hoboken, NJ: Wiley, 1996.

Karukstis, K. K., and Van Hecke, G. R. *Chemistry Connections: The Chemical Basis of Everyday Phenomena.* Burlington, MA: Academic Press, 2003.

LeMay, E. *Chemistry: Connections to Our Changing World.* New York, NY: Prentice Hall (Pearson Education), 2000.

Oxlade, C. *Elements and Compounds.* Chicago, IL: Heinemann, 2002.

Poynter, M. *Marie Curie: Discoverer of Radium **(Great Minds of Science)**.* Berkeley Heights, NJ: Enslow Publishers, 2007.

Saunders, N. *Fluorine and the Halogens.* Chicago, IL: Heinemann Library, 2005.

Shevick, E., and Wheeler, R. *Great Scientists in Action: Early Life, Discoveries, and Experiments.* Carthage, IL: Teaching and Learning Company, 2004.

Stwertka, A. *A Guide to the Elements.* New York, NY: Oxford University Press, 2002.

Tiner, J. H. *Exploring the World of Chemistry: From Ancient Metals to High-Speed Computers.* Green Forest, AZ: Master Books, 2000.

Trombley, L., and Williams, F. *Mastering the Periodic Table: 50 Activities on the Elements.* Portland, ME: Walch, 2002.

Walker, P., and Wood, E. *Crime Scene Investigations: Real-life Science Labs for Grades 6–12.* Hoboken, NJ: Jossey-Bass, 2002.

Wertheim, J. *Illustrated Dictionary of Chemistry* (Usborne Illustrated Dictionaries). Tulsa, OK: Usborne Publishing, 2000.

Wilbraham, A., et al. *Chemistry.* New York, NY: Prentice Hall (Pearson Education), 2000.

Woodford, C., and Clowes, M. *Routes of Science: Atoms and Molecules.* San Diego, CA: Blackbirch Press, 2004.

WEB SITES

The Art and Science of Bubbles
www.sdahq.org/sdakids/bubbles
*Information and activities
about bubbles.*

Chemical Achievers
www.chemheritage.org/classroom/
chemach/index.html
*Biographical details about leading
chemists and their discoveries.*

The Chemistry of Batteries
www.science.uwaterloo.ca/~cchieh/
cact/c123/battery.html
Explanation of how batteries work.

The Chemistry of Chilli Peppers
www.chemsoc.org/exemplarchem/
entries/mbellringer
*Fun site giving information on the
chemistry of chilli peppers.*

The Chemistry of Fireworks
library.thinkquest.org/15384/
chem/chem.htm
*Information on the chemical
reactions that occur when
a firework explodes.*

The Chemistry of Water
www.biology.arizona.edu/
biochemistry/tutorials/chemistry/
page3.html
*Chemistry of water and other
aspects of biochemistry.*

Chemistry: The Periodic Table Online
www.webelements.com
Detailed information about elements.

Chemistry Tutor
library.thinkquest.org/2923
*A series of Web pages that help
with chemistry assignments.*

Chem4Kids
www.chem4Kids.com
*Includes sections on matter, atoms,
elements, and biochemistry.*

Chemtutor Elements
www.chemtutor.com/elem.htm
*Information on a selection of
the elements.*

Eric Weisstein's World of Chemistry
scienceworld.wolfram.com/
chemistry
*Chemistry information divided into
eight broad topics, from chemical
reactions to quantum chemistry.*

General Chemistry Help
chemed.chem.purdue.edu/genchem
*General information on chemistry
plus movie clips of key concepts.*

Molecular Models
chemlabs.uoregon.edu/
GeneralResources/models/
models.html
*A site that explains the use
of molecular models.*

New Scientist
www.newscientist.com/home.ns
*Online science magazine providing
general news on scientific
developments.*

Periodic Tables
www.chemistrycoach.com/periodic_
tables.htm#Periodic%20Tables
*A list of links to sites that have
information on the periodic table.*

The Physical Properties of Minerals
mineral.galleries.com/minerals/
physical.htm
Methods for identifying minerals.

Understanding Our Planet Through
Chemistry
minerals.cr.usgs.gov/gips/
aii-home.htm
*Site that shows how chemists
and geologists use analytical
chemistry to study Earth.*

Scientific American
www.sciam.com
*Latest news on developments
in science and technology.*

Snowflakes and Snow Crystals
www.its.caltech.edu/~atomic/
snowcrystals
*A guide to snowflakes, snow
crystals, and other ice
phenomena.*

Virtual Laboratory: Ideal Gas Laws
zebu.uoregon.edu/nsf/piston.html
*University of Oregon site showing
simulation of ideal gas laws.*

What Is Salt?
www.saltinstitute.org/15.html
Information on common salt.

Periodic Table

The periodic table organizes all the chemical elements into a simple chart according to the physical and chemical properties of their atoms. The elements are arranged by atomic number from 1 to 116. The atomic number is based on the number of protons in the nucleus of the atom. The atomic mass is the combined mass of protons and neutrons in the nucleus. Each element has a chemical symbol that is an abbreviation of its name. In some cases, such as potassium,

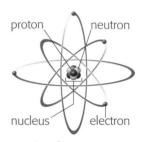

Atomic structure

33	— Atomic (proton) number
As	— Chemical symbol
Arsenic	— Element name
75	— Atomic mass

- HYDROGEN
- ALKALI METALS
- ALKALINE-EARTH METALS
- METALS
- LANTHANIDES

Transition metals

Group 1

Period 1	1 **H** Hydrogen 1

Group 2

	Group 1	Group 2	Group 3	Group 4	Group 5	Group 6	Group 7	Group 8	Group 9
Period 2	3 **Li** Lithium 7	4 **Be** Beryllium 9							
Period 3	11 **Na** Sodium 23	12 **Mg** Magnesium 24							
Period 4	19 **K** Potassium 39	20 **Ca** Calcium 40	21 **Sc** Scandium 45	22 **Ti** Titanium 48	23 **V** Vanadium 51	24 **Cr** Chromium 52	25 **Mn** Manganese 55	26 **Fe** Iron 56	27 **Co** Cobalt 59
Period 5	37 **Rb** Rubidium 85	38 **Sr** Strontium 88	39 **Y** Yttrium 89	40 **Zr** Zirconium 91	41 **Nb** Niobium 93	42 **Mo** Molybdenum 96	43 **Tc** Technetium (98)	44 **Ru** Ruthenium 101	45 **Rh** Rhodium 103
Period 6	55 **Cs** Cesium 133	56 **Ba** Barium 137	Lanthanides	72 **Hf** Hafnium 179	73 **Ta** Tantalum 181	74 **W** Tungsten 184	75 **Re** Rhenium 186	76 **Os** Osmium 190	77 **Ir** Iridium 192
Period 7	87 **Fr** Francium 223	88 **Ra** Radium 226	Actinides	104 **Rf** Rutherfordium (263)	105 **Db** Dubnium (268)	106 **Sg** Seaborgium (266)	107 **Bh** Bohrium (272)	108 **Hs** Hassium (277)	109 **Mt** Meitnerium (276)

rare-earth elements

Lanthanides

Actinides

57 **La** Lanthanum 39	58 **Ce** Cerium 140	59 **Pr** Praseodymium 141	60 **Nd** Neodymium 144	61 **Pm** Promethium (145)
89 **Ac** Actinium 227	90 **Th** Thorium 232	91 **Pa** Protactinium 231	92 **U** Uranium 238	93 **Np** Neptunium (237)

the symbol is an abbreviation of its Latin name ("K" stands for *kalium*). The name by which the element is commonly known is given in full underneath the symbol. The last item in the element box is the atomic mass. This is the average mass of an atom of the element.

Scientists have arranged the elements into vertical columns called groups and horizontal rows called periods. Elements in any one group all have the same number of electrons in their outer shell and have similar chemical properties. Periods represent the increasing number of electrons it takes to fill the inner and outer shells and become stable. When all the spaces have been filled (Group 18 atoms have all their shells filled) the next period begins. Further explanation of the periodic table is given in Volume 5.

ACTINIDES

NOBLE GASES

NONMETALS

METALLOIDS

Group 18

Group 10	Group 11	Group 12	Group 13	Group 14	Group 15	Group 16	Group 17	2 **He** Helium 4
			5 **B** Boron 11	6 **C** Carbon 12	7 **N** Nitrogen 14	8 **O** Oxygen 16	9 **F** Fluorine 19	10 **Ne** Neon 20
			13 **Al** Aluminum 27	14 **Si** Silicon 28	15 **P** Phosphorus 31	16 **S** Sulfur 32	17 **Cl** Chlorine 35	18 **Ar** Argon 40
28 **Ni** Nickel 59	29 **Cu** Copper 64	30 **Zn** Zinc 65	31 **Ga** Gallium 70	32 **Ge** Germanium 73	33 **As** Arsenic 75	34 **Se** Selenium 79	35 **Br** Bromine 80	36 **Kr** Krypton 84
46 **Pd** Palladium 106	47 **Ag** Silver 108	48 **Cd** Cadmium 112	49 **In** Indium 115	50 **Sn** Tin 119	51 **Sb** Antimony 122	52 **Te** Tellurium 128	53 **I** Iodine 127	54 **Xe** Xenon 131
78 **Pt** Platinum 195	79 **Au** Gold 197	80 **Hg** Mercury 201	81 **Tl** Thallium 204	82 **Pb** Lead 207	83 **Bi** Bismuth 209	84 **Po** Polonium (209)	85 **At** Astatine (210)	84 **Rn** Radon (222)
110 **Ds** Darmstadtium (281)	111 **Rg** Roentgenium (280)	112 **Uub** Ununbium (285)	113 **Uut** Ununtrium (284)	114 **Uuq** Ununquadium (289)	115 **Uup** Ununpentium (288)	116 **Uuh** Ununhexium (292)		

artificial elements

62 **Sm** Samarium 150	63 **Eu** Europium 152	64 **Gd** Gadolinium 157	65 **Tb** Terbium 159	66 **Dy** Dysprosium 163	67 **Ho** Holmium 165	68 **Er** Erbium 167	69 **Tm** Thulium 169	70 **Yb** Ytterbium 173	71 **Lu** Lutetium 175
94 **Pu** Plutonium (244)	95 **Am** Americium (243)	96 **Cm** Curium (247)	97 **Bk** Berkelium (247)	98 **Cf** Californium (251)	99 **Es** Einsteinium (252)	100 **Fm** Fermium (257)	101 **Md** Mendelevium (258)	102 **No** Nobelium (259)	103 **Lr** Lawrencium (260)

Glossary

acid Substance that dissolves in water to form hydrogen ions (H^+). Acids are neutralized by alkalis and have a pH below 7.

actinides Metals that with the lanthanides form the elements commonly referred to as the rare-earth metals. All actinide metals are radioactive.

alchemist Person who attempts to change one substance into another using a combination of primitive chemistry and magic.

alkali Substance that dissolves in water to form hydroxide ions (OH^-). Alkalis have a pH greater than 7 and will react with acids to form salts.

alkali metals Those metals that form Group 1 of the periodic table.

alkaline-earth metals Those metals that form Group 2 of the periodic table.

allotrope A different form of an element in which the atoms are arranged in a different structure.

alloy A metallic substance that contains two or more metals. An alloy may also be made of a metal and a small amount of a nonmetal. Steel, for example, is an alloy of iron and carbon.

amalgam Alloys that are made with mercury.

atom The smallest independent building block of matter. All substances are made of atoms.

atomic mass number The total number of protons and neutrons in an atom's nucleus.

atomic number The number of protons in a nucleus.

base A substance that produces hydroxide ions (OH^-).

boiling point The temperature at which a liquid turns into a gas.

bond The chemical connection between atoms.

brass An alloy of copper and zinc.

bronze An alloy made of copper and tin.

chemical equation Symbols and numbers that show how reactants change into products during a chemical reaction.

chemical formula The letters and numbers that represent a chemical compound, such as "H_2O" for water.

chemical reaction The reaction of two or more chemicals (the reactants) to form new chemicals (the products).

chemical symbol The letters that represent a chemical, such as "Cl" for chlorine or "Na" for sodium.

combustion The reaction that causes burning. Combustion is generally a reaction with oxygen in the air.

compound Substance made from more than one element and that has undergone a chemical reaction.

conductor A substance that carries electricity and heat well.

corrosion The slow wearing away of metals by chemical attack.

covalent bond Bond in which atoms share one or more electrons.

crystal A solid made of regular repeating patterns of atoms.

crystal lattice The regular repeated structure found in crystalline solids.

diatomic molecule Compound in which two nonmetal atoms, whether the same or different elements, are joined by the attraction of sharing electrons (covalent bonds).

dissolve To form a solution.

ductile Describes materials that can be stretched into a thin wire. Many metals are ductile.

elastic Describes a substance that returns to its original shape after being stretched.

electricity A stream of electrons or other charged particles moving through a substance.

electrolysis A method of separating elements in ionic compounds by dissolving the compound in an appropriate solvent and passing an electric current through the solution.

electromagnetic radiation The energy emitted by a source in the form of gamma rays, X-rays, ultraviolet light, visible light, infrared, microwaves, or radio waves.

electromagnetic spectrum The range of energy waves that includes light, heat, and radio waves.

electron A tiny negatively charged particle that moves around the nucleus of an atom.

electronegativity The power of an atom to attract an electron. Nonmetals, which have only a few spaces in their outer shell, are the most electronegative. Metals, which have several empty spaces, are the least electronegative. These metals will lose electrons in chemical reactions. Metals of this type arc termed electropositive.

element A material that cannot be broken up into simpler ingredients. Elements contain only one type of atom.

energy level Electron shells around an atom represent different energy levels. Those closest to the nucleus have the lowest energy.

fission Process by which a large atom breaks up into two or more smaller fragments.

four elements The ancient theory that all matter consisted of only four elements (earth, air, fire, and water) and their combinations.

fusion When small atoms fuse to make a single larger atom.

gas State in which particles are not joined and are free to move in any direction.

group A column of related elements in the periodic table.

halogens Mainly gaseous nonmetals belonging to Group 17 of the periodic table.

intermolecular bonds The bonds that hold molecules together. These bonds are weaker than those between atoms in a molecule.

intramolecular bond Strong bond between atoms in a molecule.

ion An atom that has lost or gained one or more electrons.

ionic bond Bond in which one atom gives one or more electrons to another atom.

ionization The formation of ions by adding or removing electrons from atoms.

isotope Atoms of a given element must have the same number of protons but can have different numbers of neutrons. These different versions of the same element are called isotopes.

lanthanides Metals that, with the actinides, form the elements commonly referred to as the rare-earth metals.

liquid Substance in which particles are loosely bonded and are able to move freely around each other.

malleable Describes a material that can be hammered into different shapes without breaking. Metals are malleable.

melting point The temperature at which a solid changes into a liquid. when a liquid changes into a solid, this same temperature is called the freezing point.

metal An element that is solid, shiny, malleable, ductile, and conductive.

metallic bond Bond in which outer electrons are free to move in the spaces between the atoms.

metalloid Elements that have properties of both metals and nonmetals.

mineral A natural compound that occurs in rocks and soil.

mole The amount of any substance that contains the same number of atoms as in 12 grams of carbon-12 atoms. This number is 6.022×10^{23}.

molecule Two or more joined atoms that have a unique shape and size.

neutron One of the particles that make up the nucleus of an atom. Neutrons do not have any electric charge.

noble gases A group of gases that rarely react with other elements because they have a full outer shell of electrons.

nonmetal Any element that is not a metal. Most nonmetals are gases, such as hydrogen and argon. These elements are grouped on the right-hand side of the periodic table.

nucleus The central part of an atom. The nucleus contains protons and neutrons. The exception is hydrogen, which contains only one proton.

ore A mineral that contains valuable amounts of materials such as copper, sulfur, or tin.

period A row of elements across the periodic table.

phase change A change from one state to another.

photon A particle that carries a quantity of energy, such as in the form of light.

plastic Describes a substance or material that changes shape permanently after being stretched.

pressure The force produced by pressing on something.

proton A positively charged particle found in an atom's nucleus.

radioactive decay The breakdown of an unstable nucleus through the loss of alpha and beta particles.

radiation The products of radioactivity—alpha and beta particles and gamma rays.

rare-earth metals Metals that form two rows of elements— the actinides and the lanthanides—below the main body of the periodic table.

reactivity The tendency of an element to react chemically with other elements.

relative atomic mass A measure of the mass of an atom compared with the mass of another atom. The values used are the same as those for atomic mass.

relative molecular mass The sum of all the atomic masses of the atoms in a molecule.

salt An ionic compound made by reacting an acid with an alkali.

semiconductor A substance that conducts heat and electricity but only in certain circumstances.

shell The orbit of an electron. Each shell can contain a specific number of electrons and no more.

solid State of matter in which particles are held in a rigid arrangement.

solute A substance that dissolves in a solvent.

solution A mixture of two or more elements or compounds in a single phase (solid, liquid, or gas).

solvent The liquid in which a solute dissolves.

specific heat capacity The amount of heat required to change the temperature of a specified amount of a substance by 1°C (1.8°F).

spontaneous reaction A reaction that happens by itself, without needing something else to start it off.

standard conditions Normal room temperature and pressure.

state The form that matter takes—either a solid, a liquid, or a gas.

steel An alloy of iron and carbon.

subatomic particles Particles that are smaller than an atom.

temperature A measure of how fast molecules are moving.

thiols Compounds of sulfur that often have strong or unpleasant smells.

transition metals Those metals that make up groups 3 through 12 of the periodic table.

transuranium elements Elements with an atomic number greater than that of uranium, which is 92.

valence A measure of the number of bonds an atom can form with other atoms.

valence electrons The electrons in the outer shell of an atom.

van der Waals forces Short-lived weak forces between atoms and molecules.

viscous Describes a liquid that is not very runny and flows slowly.

volume The space that a solid, liquid, or gas occupies.

wavelength The distance measured from the peak of one wave to the peak of the next wave.

Index